"This book is pure fire! In *Passionate Pursuit* Kim Owens will challenge you not just to pray for revival but to deeply and authentically experience a place in God's presence that transforms you. From that place you will become revival and bring transformation everywhere you go."

Jane Hamon, senior leader, Vision Church @ Christian International; author, *Dreams and Visions*, *The Deborah Company*, *Discernment*, *Declarations for Breakthrough*, *Confronting the Thief*

"Revival history is marked by hungry men and women of God who have pursued the fire of revival. Pastor Kim Owens is no exception. In her book, she defines with expertise and precise pointedness what passionate pursuit should look like for every believer. Let the revelation in these pages call you upward and ignite a fiery pursuit of God within you."

Judy Jacobs, copastor, Dwelling Place Church International; author, *Take It by Force!*, *Pray Until*, and more

"Kim Owens lays out a prophetic cry for every church, leader, and believer to lay aside everything and anything that would stand in the way of passionate pursuit of the manifest presence of the Lord. She defines our need for a heaven-sent revival and gives us a road map to get there."

Dr. Joe Oden, national director of prayer and evangelism, Assemblies of God; director, Assemblies of God World Prayer Center

"Pastor Kim Owens has been an incredible example to the Body of Christ of what it means to passionately pursue the Lord. For many years she has lived out the message captured in this book. I highly recommend this book as one I believe will help shape revival culture in the Church."

James Aladiran, founder, Prayer Storm

"Every once in a while God raises up a voice to call the Church back to Himself. Pastor Kim is that voice. She lives everything she's written here. Let your fire be lit by the flame from the altar she has built before God for many years."

Pastor Rick Shelton, author and speaker

PASSIONATE PURSUIT

SUSTAINING THE ZEAL OF PERSONAL REVIVAL

PASSIONATE PURSUIT

KIM OWENS

Chosen
a division of Baker Publishing Group
Minneapolis, Minnesota

Published by Chosen Books
Minneapolis, Minnesota
ChosenBooks.com

Chosen Books is a division of
Baker Publishing Group, Grand Rapids, Michigan

Library of Congress Cataloging-in-Publication Data
Names: Owens, Kim, author.
Title: Passionate Pursuit : sustaining the zeal of personal revival / Kim Owens.
Description: Minneapolis, Minnesota : Chosen Books, a division of Baker Publishing Group, 2025. | Includes bibliographical references.
Identifiers: LCCN 2024038813 | ISBN 9780800773106 (paper) | ISBN 9780800773175 (casebound) | ISBN 9781493450480 (ebook)
Subjects: LCSH: Christian life.
Classification: LCC BV4501.3 .O954 2025 | DDC 248.4—dc23/eng/20250107
LC record available at https://lccn.loc.gov/2024038813

Cover design by Peter Gloege, Look Design Studio

Baker Publishing Group publications use paper produced from sustainable forestry practices and postconsumer waste whenever possible.

25 26 27 28 29 30 31   7 6 5 4 3 2 1

I would like to dedicate this book, *Passionate Pursuit*, to my three grandchildren, Zion, Kingston, and River. It is my deepest desire to leave them with a legacy that will equip them to run their spiritual race with passion, zeal, and spiritual hunger. May they, too, carry revival to their generation and beyond as Jesus tarries.

Zion, you are the dwelling place of God. Kingston, you walk in the dominion and authority of the Lord. River, you carry the power and precious presence of the Holy Spirit. The three of you will influence nations with your mantle and anointing. Mimi loves you and dedicates this book to you. Never stop pursuing Jesus!

CONTENTS

FOREWORD

I am convinced now more than ever before that we have a desperate need for a Spirit of Revival to touch the Church and the whole nation.

Revival begins in the heart of a hungry soul who has burned every bridge, killed every lesser desire, and given their full heart to God in complete surrender.

And it's not just for a season or in your early years. Revival is a reality to be cultivated, guarded, and sustained through every season of life.

I cannot think of any person or leader in the Body of Christ who has modeled this as Kim Owens has. She has lived in sustained revival for decades and has awakened a generation to go after this same thing.

Kim's book, *Passionate Pursuit: Sustaining the Zeal of Personal Revival*, is a prophetic call to the Body of Christ to rise up and lay hold of God in a way we have not seen before.

I wholeheartedly endorse this book, and even more the author, and pray that God uses this book to awaken revival across the earth.

Corey Russell, author and speaker, CoreyRussell.org

ONE

The Power and Priority of the Place Called Secret

Revival is the result of an intentional pursuit. Desperation is the key to sustaining that pursuit. *Revival is the transformation of a life from spiritual dryness to spiritual zeal and passion for the Lord.* I have often said that the primary enemy of revival is enough. This is the state where you are comfortable and satisfied with your status quo relationship with the Lord and it hinders the critical posture of desperation required to get and keep personal revival. *Once again, revival is the return to a zeal and passion greater than you currently have.*

Since desperation is the prerequisite of a successful spiritual pursuit, we must be intentional about cultivating desperation for the Lord every day. If we don't, we will never enter revival. Logically, if we feel satisfied, we'll not be inclined to pursue anything. Pursuit is an action word that implies a passionate drive to push toward more than you currently have. There is always more of God to experience.

A mindset of enough convinces you that more is not necessary or available. This is not the perspective of a desperate person. Desperation speaks of extreme **The primary** measures and behavior to satisfy an area of **enemy of revival** desire or need. Naturally speaking, this could **is enough.** be the satisfaction of hunger and thirst. In the spiritual realm, it is the same. Our spiritual pursuit creates hunger and thirst, which, in turn, creates desperation for more. This powerful cycle leads us into a deepening relationship with the Lord. In the cry of David, we get insight into a desperate heart. "O God, You are my God; early will I seek You; my soul thirsts for You; my flesh longs for You in a dry and thirsty land where there is no water" (Psalm 63:1).

Can you hear the desperation and the intentional pursuit to satisfy that cry? Like David, every believer should have and keep a passionate spiritual pursuit of God. This pursuit must consume our lives. It should be the first thing on our mind in the morning, and it should be in our thoughts all throughout the day. A personal revival begins and continues with a passionate pursuit of God: His presence, His person, and His purposes. If you truly desire this, you must live in the state of desperately longing for God.

Because we so easily settle for empty religious activity, which is form without power, appearance without substance, talk without walk, fanfare without fire, and excitement without authority, we operate without the vital posture of desperation. Why do you need desperation when everything is only a façade? It takes no hunger or desire to live a status

14

quo spiritual life. We can easily fill our lives with spiritual activity and assume this is growing our spiritual capacity when in reality it is only consuming vital time and spiritual energy that could be used in passionate pursuit of His presence. Working for the Lord is biblical; however, doing so out of an empty spiritual well is dangerous.

> Personal revival comes with the demand of being able to sustain credible hunger for more.

Too many have settled for aesthetics or ornamental Christianity while God is looking for zealous longing. We've become polished while God wants purity, and we work hard on performance while God wants heartfelt passion.

Personal revival comes with the demand of being able to sustain credible hunger for more, a desperate aching for spiritual change, and a deep longing for Him. You must develop the discipline of staying desperate. I call it *the discipline of the desperate*!

Discipline is the ability to cultivate a behavior and habit that allows you to sustain a standard. So cultivating and sustaining the yearning and longing for God daily is what your personal revival pursuit is all about. The byproduct is a life lived in the fullness of His presence. It is a life lived alive, on fire, and with zeal and passion for the heart of God. Every notable historical revival began with a person or a company of people who were desperate for more. They came to a place where they realized that what they had was not enough, and they would not settle for a nominal level of spiritual pursuit. It is out of these passionate hearts where people stayed desperate that we read historical accounts of territories, governments, and nations forever being altered by revival.

15

What about you? Will that be your story? I want it to be mine. Not just for myself, but for my children and grandchildren. If Jesus tarries, I want to leave a legacy of spiritual desperation. One that testifies of a pursuit of God in which I did not settle. Let this be your story, too.

This book will walk you through vital revelations and principles to empower your desperation for God and your pursuit of revival. I pray that you will be changed, challenged, and equipped to have a tenacious pursuit of God. The first place that you begin is the place called secret.

There will be no personal revival if there is no spiritual pursuit. At the beginning of this book, you must answer the question, "Is spiritual pursuit a priority in my life?" A constant goal of the desperate seeker is the ongoing pursuit of God and His presence pressing into more of God to develop a deep, intimate relationship with Him. Revival is the result of a desperation that drives constant spiritual pursuit.

You don't accidentally walk into revival. It is sought, dug out, and plowed. It is a spiritual transaction that can only be accessed by spiritual pursuit. There must be continual breaking of the fallow or uncultivated ground of your heart to make sure that it is tilled and ready for the seeds of the Spirit to be planted. Those seeds bring forth greater spiritual maturity, which leads you to ongoing hunger for the Lord. The primary place of pursuit for personal revival is your personal secret place.

Jesus speaks of this special place available to us. "When you pray, go into your room, and when you have shut your door, pray to your Father who is in the secret place; and your Father who sees in secret will reward you openly" (Matthew 6:6).

The Word is clear that the secret place is where the Father dwells. Pause for a moment and think about that one amazing detail. The Father dwells in the secret place, and when you go there, He meets you, hears you, and communes with you!

The Bible also tells us that God sees you there. This means that He also sees when you're *not* there. I am convinced that many do not have a deep revelation of the importance of the secret place because they fail to realize that the Father created the place and that He's always waiting for you to enter. He's waiting for you to go into the room, shut the door, and pray. You have an assurance that He's always there. What a monumental privilege we have in the place called secret.

> The primary place of pursuit for personal revival is your personal secret place.

There has been much said about Matthew 6:6 with wonderful, practical, and spiritual insights into the personal secret place. But I cannot leave this verse without noting that we're specifically told by Jesus to pray, to have a room, and to shut the door. This verse assumes that we have these things in place and in order in our lives. Hear what the Spirit is saying: You should have a designated room or space, and you should commit to an intentional time set aside where the door is shut and distractions are closed out so that you can pray and meet the Father who is waiting for you.

If there is this level of intentionality in the Word of God about the secret place, we must have ears to hear how important this is to personal revival. Without it, we digress spiritually. Jesus didn't say *if* you pray, He said *when* you pray. Your prayer appointment is the most important meeting you have every day. It should not be an option or an add-on after you complete other activities or duties. It should be prioritized above all else.

Jesus modeled this for us throughout His ministry on earth. "Very early in the morning, while it was still dark, Jesus got up, left the house and went off to a solitary place, where he prayed" (Mark 1:35 NIV). And the psalmist instructed us to prioritize this every day. "I rise before dawn and cry for help; I have put my hope in your word" (Psalm 119:147 NIV).

When the secret place is inactive, we grow stagnant, stale, and stifled. Spiritual pursuit breaks spiritual stagnation and leads you into greater intimacy and spiritual authority. To what are you giving yourself? Where are your priorities? In what areas of your life have you spent the most time disciplining yourself? It is truly worth evaluating so that you can have an honest assessment of your loyalties.

We're all pursuing something. Do you check your social media before you check into the secret place? Are you distracted from your time with the Father by outside attractions that appeal to your flesh or your intellect? Is the first thing on your mind in the morning all the activities or responsibilities that you have for the day? Stop and think about all that you're giving yourself to before you choose the Lord. This is idolatry, and it is keeping you from personal revival. This was not how Jesus operated. His appointment with His Father was His lifeline for spiritual fulfillment and for success in all that He did in life and ministry. It should be ours as well.

Pursuit of other things is not necessarily wrong unless those things are sinful. Even good things can take the place of your time dedicated to personal spiritual pursuit. Jesus made a clear directive that seeking the Kingdom of God was to be the priority in our lives. "But seek (aim at and strive after) first of all His kingdom and His righteousness (His way of doing and being right), and then all these things taken together will be given you besides" (Matthew 6:33 AMPC).

This verse shows the urgency with which we should be placing priority on pursuit of the Kingdom. It also shows us that everything else that we are concerned with will be taken care of if we will only prioritize the Kingdom!

Even good things can take the place of your time dedicated to personal spiritual pursuit.

We are instructed all throughout the Word of God to pursue things of eternal value. So we must determine to *put the secret place above every other place* in our lives. Colossians 3:1–2 (AMPC), gives us insight as to what this looks like:

> If then you have been raised with Christ [to a new life, thus sharing His resurrection from the dead], aim at *and* seek the [rich, eternal treasures] that are above, where Christ is, seated at the right hand of God. And set your minds and keep them set on what is above (the higher things), not on the things that are on the earth.

We must also be aware of any wrong pursuits that hinder our spiritual pursuit, make adjustments in our lives regardless of the level of sacrifice, and begin to pursue the higher things. This and only this is the primary entry point and sustaining point to personal revival.

"He who dwells in the secret place of the Most High shall abide under the shadow of the Almighty" (Psalm 91:1).

Passionate Pursuit

There is a special place where personal revival is cultivated and maintained. It is called secret not because God doesn't want you to know about it or where it is, but because it is a place reserved for you to daily begin your spiritual walk with Him. The desperate not only know how to find it but also long to live in it. He who dwells, takes up residence, in the secret place abides, stays, under the shadow of the Almighty. This is the power of the place called secret.

A gripping reality is that the level of revival in every corporate atmosphere is released by the level of revival in our personal atmosphere. As a revivalist and a pastor, I often tell people, "You bring your secret place into this place (the church)." Revival truly begins in the individual heart. Evangelist Gipsy Smith was asked what the secret of revival is. He said, "Go home. Take a piece of chalk. Draw a circle around yourself. Then pray, 'O Lord, revive everything inside this circle.'"[1]

Inside that circle, you can't imagine the divine exchange that will take place. Your heart will be transformed, and you will become a new person. You'll be a better spouse, parent, employee, business owner, and church attendee. Mostly, you will have an intimate relationship with Jesus, which is the highest privilege that we've been given.

Protect the time that you spend in this place. Shut out all distractions and begin your personal revival walk, daily. Remember, the Father sees you! If this doesn't make you desperate for this place, I don't know what will. The Father then rewards you openly because you made sure that you found the place where the walk begins—it's the place called secret.

This pursuit never ends. You're preparing for eternity. Every day is a new encounter with an eternal God. How can there be an arrival time or destination when the pursuit is eternal? One day we will step from time to eternity and this pursuit will take on an entirely different stride. One that we can't fully describe inside the confines of time, but one that will propel us through unending realms of glory discovering unending revelations of God.

The success of your personal secret place will be fueled by an eternal perspective. As you realize each day that you're preparing for an eternal pursuit, you'll be strengthened and built up to persevere, your capacity will expand, and your connection of intimacy will be deepened.

Our time to start is now. The way we leave this earth is the way we will begin in heaven. Oh, how our longing should be heightened every day to get to that place called secret. This is what we were born for. This is what we were made for! There is no greater honor than to have been given a special secret place. He'll meet you there tomorrow. Be sure to meet with Him!

TWO

Where Are You?
Revival Is a Walk!

It cannot be ignored that God walked with Adam and Eve. The following verse is our first example of His pursuit of us.

> And they heard the sound of the Lord God walking in the garden in the cool of the day, and Adam and his wife hid themselves from the presence of the Lord God among the trees of the garden. But the Lord God called to Adam and said to him, Where are you? He said, I heard the sound of You [walking] in the garden, and I was afraid because I was naked; and I hid myself.
>
> Genesis 3:8–10 AMPC

I'm not quite sure how I have read over this verse so many times without realizing that Adam and Eve had intimate and personal fellowship with Creator God that was at God's

23

bidding every day. This is mind-blowing. An invitation by God to walk.

Revival is a walk. It is not a sprint but rather a disciplined walk with God that grows sweeter and more glorious every day; however, we must submit to the walk. This passage is gripping. When God asks a question, it is not because He needs an answer, it is because He wants us to locate where we are. *Adam, where are you?* Possibly this was to draw Adam's attention to his neglect.

It should be noted that God misses our walks when we don't show up. He pursues us and asks us by name where we are. This is how passionate God is that we *live in* the state of revival; the spiritual state of awakening and zeal for Him and His presence. I don't ever want to be found in a place where God must ask where I am.

The desperate person will discipline themselves to walk every day. It is an exercise that began in the Garden and is still on God's agenda every day. Revival is a walk. A passionate pursuit. God is still walking. Are you? "With passion I pursue and cling to you. Because I feel your grip on my life, I keep my soul close to your heart" (Psalm 63:8 TPT).

In the last chapter, we covered the power and priority of pursuit. If we do not prioritize pursuit, we will grow stagnant. This brings a greater understanding as to why God wanted to walk every day with His creation. The passage in Genesis that we began with is where we get the understanding that Adam walked with God in fellowship in the Garden. There was unhindered, unbroken, uninhibited fellowship and communion with Creator God.

This walk was and still is *intentional* for the Lord. He wants to see your consistent commitment to Him, the cultivation of your love for Him, and your desire to honor and worship Him. This is why revival is a deliberate spiritual walk, one that has intentionality and purpose. The purpose is His, which is why the walk never ceases. Every revival step has a reason. Our core spiritual capacity increases as we stretch with the stride of God. The longer we walk with Him the more we look like Him! Isn't that the

> Our core spiritual capacity increases as we stretch with the stride of God.

goal? "But we all, with unveiled face, beholding as in a mirror the glory of the Lord, are being transformed into the same image from glory to glory, just as by the Spirit of the Lord" (2 Corinthians 3:18).

This walk called revival means personal relationship, intimacy, and spiritual pursuit. It is very important to note that the walk cannot be replaced by any other activity or spiritual exercise. It's an intentional revival walk of desperation. That's it. If we start replacing the walk with other activities or loyalties, we end up with religion, not relationship. Talk without the walk. The apostle Paul expresses the deep level of intimacy to which I am describing:

> Yet indeed I also count all things loss for the excellence of the knowledge of Christ Jesus my Lord . . . that I may gain Christ and be found in Him . . . that I may know Him and the power of His resurrection, and the fellowship of His sufferings, being conformed to His death.
>
> Philippians 3:8–10

The Revival Study Bible mentions this train of thought as well.

25

The highest calling known to man is the call to intimacy with God. All others stand in direct opposition to it and become idols if intimacy with God takes second place . . . this requires a pursuit, and this pursuit is called a walk.[1]

Strong's Concordance tells us that in Hebrew, the meaning of *walk* is "continually." In the Greek language, the meaning of *walk* is "to be occupied with." I've also heard it referred to like this: addicted to a pursuit.[2]

The emphasis is on the walk. "And they heard the sound of the Lord God walking." God didn't intend for this sound to decrease or this walk to end. Revival is hearing the continual walking footsteps of God and joining with Him. If this is to be a reality in your personal life, you'll need to learn the walk. Again, this walk is intimacy with the Lord. We must guard against simply doing Christian or Church things and replacing walking with God with those things. These things may be important and necessary, but they are peripheral to the walk.

If you don't keep walking, you're going to lose revival. It's one thing to start a fire, but it's an entirely different process and cost to keep it burning. Count the cost! It cannot become anything more or less than the walk. You can't get bored. You can't recreate. You can't reroute. You can't add to. You must keep walking. Revival is a walk that is intended to increase in intensity and glory, and it is to last forever. Pace yourself and learn to hear the sound of the Lord God walking.

I say this with a gripping conviction: It is a pure pursuit that sustains the walk. Whatever you must do to stay in pursuit, that is what you must do. Nothing is worth compromising the walk of following after Him. You must become aware that at any moment your last encounter can become a religious monument if you do not keep pursuing, if you do not keep walking.

He recognizes our absence. If we stop responding to His walk, we, too, may hear the question *Adam, where are you?* Adam heard the sound, and he went absent. The Spirit will always prompt us to continue the walk, daily. It is our choices that determine if the walk is successful. God always shows up. Do you? Don't miss the walk. If the walk ceases, the result is shame. "I heard Your voice in the garden, and I was afraid because I was naked; and I hid myself" (Genesis 3:9–10).

> Nothing is worth compromising the walk of following after Him.

It is astonishing to know that God missed walking with Adam. If for no other reason, I should be compelled to go to the secret place because I know that God will miss our time. When I don't show up, He asks, *Where are you?* Sadly, this is the case too much of the time. Form without passion and power is where religion takes over. The right talk but without the walk. Excitement but without spiritual authority found in walking in intimacy with God.

Religion doesn't require a walk—it's all talk. We talk about the walk, but we don't *actually walk*. The walk of Genesis 3 was to be an eternal walk that started in the Garden and never ended. Because Jesus walked the hill to Golgotha, the original no-show of Adam has been replaced with an eternal invitation to walk. You see, God never stopped walking, and He still walks today. He longs to meet us at the spiritual Eden for an encounter with His intimate fellowship, to witness

His glory, and to breathe in His creation. He longs for that walk. Do you?

The walk is strenuous and costly. It's not a leisurely stroll, it's a focused preoccupation with Him, not yourself. It is an addiction to pursuing Him, not selfish ambitions. It was always intended to be a sustained walk, and it costs a lot to sustain His presence. It costs nothing to sustain religion, just do or don't do what you want or don't want to do, that's easy and that's religion. But the walk will cost you everything.

Can you imagine? They heard the sound of the walk of God! They knew the intimacy of His sound. They knew the power and the authority of His walk. They knew that His walk was a call to fellowship, a call to glory, and a call to connect with their Creator. His walk was their sustenance and their substance. It was their satisfaction, their frequency, and their cadence. They knew no other, nor did they desire any other sound or rhythm. Just the walk. Every day. No headlines needed, no super-duper post or marketing strategy. This was what normal was supposed to be. Every day was a walk with God!

Could it be possible that even in the perfection of the Garden of Eden this walk became so normal for them that they took advantage of the privilege to walk? It became mundane and nominal. It is incredibly overwhelming to understand how much responsibility we have to stir ourselves in our spiritual pursuit. Any spiritual discipline can become mundane, but it is in the mundane that miracle moments happen.

Think about the ten days in the Upper Room. Sure, Jesus told them to go and tarry, but they didn't know exactly for what they were tarrying, nor did they know how long they would need to tarry. They didn't have the full picture—only a directive of Jesus. What if they had left the room on day eight or nine? They would have missed the prophetic outpouring promised from long ago. What do you miss when you miss your walk?

Revival is a walk, an addictive pursuit, and it may have explosive moments of glory. There may be moments that require everything within you to pull on His realm or to take an aggressive stance of grabbing hold of God and bringing Him closer, but it is all a part of the walk.

And every moment of walking with Him is its own reward. It is such a privilege to walk with Him. Above all other sounds, may we hear the sound of God walking. It's a continual, unending, perpetual call to fellowship. True personal revival is pursuing Him as you would a craving. It is an addiction to pursuing His presence that outweighs and outshines all other pursuits. When you're addicted to something, you are devoted to and dependent on it.

We've been conditioned to boosters that cause us to become immune to the long-term sustainability of the revival walk. This is a problem that must be addressed. What is a booster? A booster is something that will improve or increase but is not sustainable. In the context of spiritual pursuit, we must depend primarily on our personal discipline to walk with God, while using boosters as an add-on. We should not become dependent upon boosters in lieu of our daily walk.

At some point you will need another dose of the same booster. What are some of the boosters that we ride on instead of taking the walk? In our day, social media is a huge culprit. There are podcasts, interviews, and videos short and long that take our time away from the personal walk. These things can be a help along the way if the content is sound, but they should never replace the walk. Remember, it's intimate and personal between you and God. He doesn't need any help; He just needs you to show up. How is it that we've learned to do so many things *without the walk* when the only thing that God really wants is *to walk*? He's still asking, "Where are you?"

The results of the revival walk are determined by God. You cannot put an expectation on the walk. It is God who chooses which side of Himself He desires to show you. He decides which revelation He will unveil, and He decides which level of glory you get to walk through on the pursuit. This is dictated by His assessment of what you're ready to encounter. But one thing is for sure, He never disappoints! This is why there are different types of revivals, which include healing, repentance, prayer, etc. God never runs out of revelation and glory. He is eternal, and His supply is endless and limitless. This is why we must keep walking.

Yet we're so easily diverted and distracted. Satan's diversions, detours, and distractions come through many avenues. One of those is a spirit of perversion. It is a twisting of God's original desire and design. These perversions are ready to interrupt the walk and cause us to become addicted to a lesser pursuit. The enemy is subtle, just as he was with Eve. He has learned how to package perversion in spiritual language that makes us think we're still walking with God. In reality, though, we are just on a hamster wheel of self-focused frenzy.

An age-old temptation is that if you can't get people to stop walking, make them run; therefore, many turn the walk into a race, and life becomes a rat race. A rat race is a way of life in which people are caught up in a fiercely competitive struggle for wealth, power, and popularity. That competition is exhausting.

In the Garden of Eden, they traded the walk for a race—a rat race. The moment they made the trade is the moment the race began and the walk ended. Remember, the walk is about intimacy, so the perversion or twisting of that would be a race that is only about separation, detachment, and aloofness. Satan's goal is to get you focused more on what you get out of the relationship rather than the fact that you have the privilege to walk with your Creator.

Yes, Paul gave us the illustration of a race in our Christian pursuit; however, the way Paul uses the example of running a race is within the context of discipline.

> Do you not know that those who run in a race all run, but one receives the prize? Run in such a way that you may obtain it. And everyone who competes for the prize is temperate in all things. Now they do it to obtain a perishable crown, but we for an imperishable crown. Therefore I run thus: not with uncertainty. Thus I fight: not as one who beats the air. But I discipline my body and bring it into subjection, lest, when I have preached to others, I myself should become disqualified.
>
> 1 Corinthians 9:24–27

The context in this passage is not speed or competition. He speaks of physical discipline and of a perishable versus imperishable crown. This is vastly different from a rat race that is a fiercely competitive struggle.

In the natural, the rat race is driven by money, popularity, and success. You don't have to strip away many layers of spiritual talk before you find this same motivation for self-worth in the Church. Religion has perverted the walk, so we run fast to see who can produce the most and shine the brightest. Thus, the hamster wheel of religious activity.

Did you know that hamsters can experience wheel addiction? "Just like people, hamsters can get addicted to things. . . . They can also get addicted to the exercise wheel."[3] If there are no other options (toys or equipment) in your hamster's cage, they can get bored, which they will solve by spending too much time on the wheel.

Through a religious spirit, the devil has made sure that we only have one piece of equipment in the cage of religion. That piece of equipment, whatever it may look like, will always be centered around us. It will release a striving spirit that sends you into a frenzied addiction to keep going even though you're not going anywhere. Hamster wheel. This is religion.

Are you addicted to the religious rat race or to the revival pursuit? These are two very different things. A true revival walk will not be one of popularity. If success comes your way, it is only because God has allowed you to help others get off the wheel and back on the walk. Revival is not about success. The revivalists of old did not have popularity in their minds. They simply had a revelation of the walk. The byproduct of the walk was that people wanted to follow them as they followed Christ. In other words, a true revivalist will walk in such a manner that others will join them. Oh, that we would have a true revelation of the power of the walk!

The rat race gives the effect and affirmation that you're walking, when you're only just spinning—but it can be addictive. Make sure you're on the walk and not the wheel. The revival walk is one of labor: revelatory labor, consecration labor, dying-to-self labor, and warfare labor. It is never-ending labor. So the wheel and the race begin to look good in comparison to the sacrifice of the walk.

It is unfortunate that when we grow weary of the walk, we concede that it's easier to just join the race. And this is where you find many people, which is the same place that Satan left Adam

> A true revivalist will walk in such a manner that others will join them.

and Eve in the Garden of Eden. They accepted a substitute for the walk of eternity.

Let me reel this in again toward our goal that *revival is a walk*. It is an addiction to a pursuit of Him, and anything that impedes, distracts, or diverts us from this core purpose is not revival. And anything we find affirmation or satisfaction in other than this core purpose is not revival. The appearance of pursuit and the addiction to pursuit are two very opposite things. Jesus made a way for us to get off the wheel and back on the walk. The sound of the walk in the Garden echoes through the cross. The torn veil is God walking through the barrier and confinement of religion to reach a heart that wants to walk again.

I believe the wheel and race we face today is still religion; talk without the walk. What motivates me to write is a fierce zeal to protect the purity of the walk. Don't run on that wheel and call it revival. Do the sacrificial training to stay on the walk. Do you truly desire to keep personal revival alive in your life? How's your stamina for the walk that never ends? This is what it will take. You can do it. It is possible—not easy, but possible. The first thing you must do is get a deep revelation of the walk that began in the Garden, was lost in the Garden, then won again in another garden. What God has always desired is to walk with you, and this is revival.

King David earned the reputation of being a man after God's own heart (see 1 Samuel 13:14). If you closely observe his life, he was less than perfect, but he was pure. Even after sins that grieved the heart of God, he was able to find forgiveness and prioritize his life in pursuit of one thing.

> One thing have I asked of the Lord, that will I seek, inquire for, and [insistently] require: that I may dwell in the house of the Lord [in His presence] all the days of my life, to behold and gaze upon the beauty [the sweet attractiveness and the delightful loveliness] of the Lord and to meditate, consider, and inquire in His temple.
>
> Psalm 27:4 AMPC

David had a revelation of the walk, and this passion won him a place in God's heart. God, therefore, determined never to let David's legacy be forgotten. Those who choose the walk will always receive the endorsement of God. If we learn to trust in that reality, we will get off the wheel and out of the race. I implore you, don't stop short.

David was a man after God's own heart. He sacrificed to get the Ark of the Covenant back to Jerusalem. He prioritized personal worship. He taught people how to release it. This is the tabernacle that the Lord said He would restore (see Amos 9:11 and Acts 15:16). Why? It was his heart of pursuit that caught the attention of God more than any other form of worship in the Old Testament.

David had proven that he would walk with God, whether on a hill with some sheep or on a throne with a crown. He'd proven that nothing would keep him from bringing honor to the presence of the Lord. Battles would be fought and giants would be slain because a constant walk was driving David's zeal for the Lord, His house, and His presence. As you read his psalms, you hear the footsteps of the walk within each word. There's no doubt as to why David was a man after God's own heart. He understood the walk.

The same is true today. Those who follow God's heart understand the walk. They will do whatever it takes to stay in shape to keep walking, no matter what. Revival is a walk. For some of you, it's time to start walking again. For others, be encouraged to keep walking. Stay on the walk. This is where God began; it is what Jesus restored. The choice is yours.

THREE

The Revelation of More

Every notable revival began with a revelation of more. Those at Azusa Street held to the promise of the baptism in the Holy Spirit; the Hebrides revival held to the promise of an outpouring of spiritual water on dry spiritual ground; the Welsh revival held to a promise of His manifested presence through prayer; and the Brownsville revival held to a promise of revival fire unto deep repentance.

A revelation is an unveiling of the mind that has been blinded or darkened to truths of God. At the point of revelation, the spirit of a man comes alive by the Spirit of God, and what was once obscure and unsure is now clear and conscious.

For revival to be born in a heart or a people, someone must reach the point of a revelation of more. If not, you will be content to stay in the lesser. This revelation takes us past our superficial spiritual exercises and temporal understanding, knowledge, or intelligence into a revelation of more of God.

We serve a God of infinitude. He is limitless. If God is limitless, then there must be more!

What if it is not real mansions that Jesus went to prepare for us but rooms or places of revelation about Him and His eternity? This was the question prompted in my spirit as I read the verse spoken by Jesus. "My Father's house has many rooms; if that were not so, would I have told you that I am going there to prepare a place for you?" (John 14:2 NIV).

What if throughout eternity we are in one room or place receiving revelation(s) of God and Who He is for an undetermined amount of time? And when we think we've learned it all, the angels escort us into yet another room or place of revelation to receive more unveiling of Him? I am not trying to create another doctrine, but I do believe this is what the Word teaches as we look at the progression of degrees of glory.

> And all of us, as with unveiled face, [because we] continued to behold [in the Word of God] as in a mirror the glory of the Lord, are constantly being transfigured into His very own image in ever increasing splendor and from one degree of glory to another; [for this comes] from the Lord [Who is] the Spirit.
>
> 2 Corinthians 3:18 AMPC

This verse says that we go from one degree of glory to another degree of glory. If we can do that now, it wouldn't be a far reach to say that we will be doing that for eternity. But the key to this thought and the point of this chapter is that we *can* go from one degree of glory to another. So the prevailing question is, why would we only want to stay at one degree? If there is more glory, which is more of God, why wouldn't we want to pursue this?

Personal revival that is sustained has a desperate longing to grow from glory to glory. That continues until we leave this place called time, and we transition into an eternity of worshiping, learning, knowing, and loving more of Him forever. It is very difficult for us to wrap our minds around this, which is why we must lift our eyes from the temporal to the eternal.

We must cut all ties to the temporal that keep us from viewing our walk with God through the lens of eternity. This is what we will be doing . . . forever. Worship is not a set of songs that are sung just before the preacher preaches. Worship is the life we live for God, and it is the only reason we are here. We are getting ready for *there*! The desperate ones get a head start on it now.

The revelation of more is at the core of desperate seekers. They are thankful for everything they have encountered yet are not satisfied. The revelation of more has taught them that with one more step on the walk they will walk into more.

Again, religion has taught us to be satisfied with the aesthetics of Christianity. If I am fulfilling the duties and checking the boxes, I'm good. Right? Well, yes in the sense that you are being obedient to the Lord in a call or a commission, but what about the substance behind that call and commission? This is where the revelation of more becomes crucial in revival to differentiate between the appearance of Christ and the substance of Christ. You can learn *about* Him, but you cannot *become* Him until you're *around* Him!

> Worship is the life we live for God, and it is the only reason we are here.

The company you keep determines the culture you create. This is true in human relationships, and it is true in our spiritual relationship with the Lord. The more time I spend with Him, the more I create *a Jesus culture* in my life. Not a church culture. While being involved in a church is very important to be a healthy Christian, what is a greater priority is that Christ is in my Christianity. The only way for this to happen is to make sure that Christ is the primary company that I keep.

It was said by the religious leaders to Peter and the early apostles that they were shocked at what the apostles carried spiritually because the religious leaders knew them to be uneducated men (see Acts 4:13). But their indictment was they could tell that Peter and John had been with Jesus. Can others tell you have been with Jesus? If there is an indictment to be had, it would be this one. You look, act, talk, and walk just like Jesus.

Do you want people to see that you carry something? What is this something? It is the authority, ability, weight, and power that Jesus carried. "And they were amazed at His teaching, for His word was with authority and ability and weight and power" (Luke 4:32 AMPC). People could not resist His words, because they came from another realm that countered and challenged the limited realm in which they existed.

For far too long, the Church has been operating from the temporal realm to the neglect of the eternal realm. We plan our church programs, ministries, and events around the temporal. The primary reason this is done is to attract people. And the primary reason it has worked for so long is because many people have a deficit of ability, authority, weight, and power from the supernatural realm. It is time to get back to the indictment of the early apostles: We can tell you've been with Jesus. The company you keep will be the type of indictment you receive. The atmosphere you entertain will be the atmosphere you carry.

The pursuit of believers and entire churches has been halted because of the lack of revelation of more. The Bible tells us:

> For He whom God has sent speaks the words of God; for He gives the Spirit without measure.
>
> John 3:34 NASB

> After these things I looked, and behold, a door standing open in heaven, and the first voice which I had heard, like the sound of a trumpet speaking with me, said, "Come up here, and I will show you what must take place after these things."
>
> Revelation 4:1 NASB

> But just as it is written, "Things which eye has not seen and ear has not heard, and which have not entered the heart of man, all that God has prepared for those who love Him."
>
> 1 Corinthians 2:9 NASB

> Call to Me and I will answer you, and I will tell you great and mighty things, which you do not know.
>
> Jeremiah 33:3 NASB

Listen to what the Word just showed us. We are promised the Spirit without measure. He will show us things that must take place. Our eyes have not seen all that God has prepared for us, and He will tell us great and mighty things that we do not know! Yet we stop or limit our pursuit because we think that God has tapped out. God does not tap out—we do.

God does not tap out—we do.
These are only a few of the Bible passages that speak of the untapped mysteries of God. I fully understand that there are some things that we will not know or encounter until we get to heaven, but I equally understand that it is the glory of kings to search things out and that deep calls unto deep.

> But just as it is written, "Things which eye has not seen and ear has not heard, and which have not entered the heart of man, all that God has prepared for those who love Him." For to us God revealed them through the Spirit; for the Spirit searches all things, even the depths of God. For who among men knows the thoughts of a man except the spirit of the man which is in him? Even so the thoughts of God no one knows except the Spirit of God. Now we have received, not the spirit of the world, but the Spirit who is from God, so that we may know the things freely given to us by God, which things we also speak, not in words taught by human wisdom, but in those taught by the Spirit, combining spiritual thoughts with spiritual words.
>
> 1 Corinthians 2:9–13

If the Spirit is searching the depths of God and revealing His thoughts and plans to us, why do we stop at shallow searches? The primary reason is because we feel we have enough. But desperate seekers have a revelation of more. They believe that eternity is calling from the secret place of His presence what eyes have not yet seen. Because of this, an occasional encounter with God is not enough for desperate seekers. We must pursue Him with everything within us until we collide with the more.

Come near to the holy men and women of the past and you will soon feel the heat of their desire after God. They mourned for Him, they prayed and wrestled and sought for Him day and night, in season and out, and when they had found Him the finding was all the sweeter for the long seeking.

A. W. Tozer; *The Pursuit of God*[1]

The revelation of more swings on doors that lead us to more. In many cases, however, we have stopped swinging these doors. Remember how I began this chapter? What if throughout eternity we are in one room receiving revelation(s) of God and Who He is for an undetermined amount of time, and just when we think we have learned it all, the angels escort us into yet another room of revelation to receive more unveiling of Him? The door to these rooms of revelation must stay active in our spiritual pursuit. If they do not, the hinges become rusty, we become stagnant, and eventually we stop our pursuit.

Rusty hinges!! There have been doors that have been locked down for decades. God is going to use you to open them. God is going to open doors because we've been locked out of so much! Rusty hinges! Rusty hinges!

John Kilpatrick, a wonderful, trusted, and anointed general of the historic Brownsville revival, spoke these words to me during one of our Doorkeepers of Revival weekends. I must admit that when he gave the initial release of this word of the Lord, I was perplexed as to what the Lord meant by rusty hinges. But it was such a specific word that

I began to pray into it. I felt the Lord say, *The hinges are rusty because the doors are dormant.* Remember, we're speaking about spiritual doors to more. More of God, more of His Spirit, and more of His presence, authority, and power.

In the context of revival, I am convinced that rusty hinges are the reason we experience dry atmospheres and dead church services that are void of the glory of the Lord. Rusty hinges are the byproduct of systems and structures that only build a ministry but don't birth spiritual outpouring. Rusty hinges are the result of preachers who have become parrots of cultural nuisances. It is much easier to google a sermon topic than it is to fast and pray for a revelation. It is much easier to copy and paste than it is to dig spiritual wells by hours of reading the Word and ingesting it until it becomes *rhema* unto revelation.

Rusty hinges are the result of people who *go* to church instead of *being* the Church. Rusty hinges are the result of settling for a religious activity instead of a revival encounter. This is the sad state of much of the American Church, and the result is rusty hinges.

Spiritual doors cannot swing on their own. They swing on the desperation and spiritual hunger of those who do not want to miss the supernatural, the Spirit, the oil, and the wine. And the man of God said to me by the Spirit of God, "They've been locked down for decades. Rusty hinges!" When you stop swinging doors, you cancel your access to more of God. We cannot ignore the door to more!

Doors swing on hinges. It is gripping to note that a small hinge to the door of His presence is noted in the book of 1 Kings.

Thus Solomon had all the furnishings made for the house of the Lord: the altar of gold, and the table of gold . . . the lampstands of pure gold . . . and the lamps and the wick-trimmers of gold; the basins, the trimmers, the bowls, the ladles, and the censers of pure gold; and the hinges of gold, both for the doors of the inner room (the Most Holy Place) and for the doors of the main hall of the temple.

1 Kings 7:48–50

The prophetic word given to me said that the hinges have become rusty. The hinges that swing the door to His thick presence have become neglected and corroded, and this has produced the irritating sound of creaking and croaking anytime we approach the door. These sounds have kept revival and the glory out that are contained beyond the door. Religion tells us that it is too much work to deal with those hinges, and that sound is just too offensive. Who has the time, spiritual depth, or cares to do what it takes to get the oil for those hinges, anyway? We have got a quicker, more current way that has the appearance that we're swinging doors. But where do those doors lead?

Our resolution is that there are other doors we can choose from. These doors have much easier access and new hinges that are in perfect working order. They are, however, doors that lead to nowhere! Behind these doors are empty rooms void of presence. At least we're swinging doors, right? This is the voice of the enemy that keeps us from the revelation of more.

In our modern Church culture, the enemy has convinced many seekers to pursue doors to nowhere. Some of these doors are doors of reconstruction. Deconstructionists are propagating doctrines of demons that take established doctrine and faith and deconstruct them to fit carnality and compromise. Yet the Bible clearly tells us to not move boundary stones. "Do not move an ancient boundary stone set up by your ancestors" (Proverbs 22:28).

We are to ask for the ancient paths, the godly ways, and then walk (pursue) those paths. "This is what the LORD says: 'Stop at the crossroads and look around. Ask for the old, godly way, and walk in it. Travel its path, and you will find rest for your souls. But you reply, "No, that's not the road we want!"'" (Jeremiah 6:16 NLT).

Then there is the cultural door. This door leads us to feel as though we must swing doors that culture has created and incorporate them into our Christian lives and church services. These are doors of mixture that cause confusion to the unsaved and dilute the pure presence and Word of God in our lives. The Word of God is clear that we are to come out from among them and be separate (see 2 Corinthians 6:17).

And then there is the door of compromise—compromise of biblical standards of holiness. Yet as we swing this door, it is as if we are looking the other way at sin and iniquity. Where are those today like Phinehas who watch the door? Phinehas protected holiness at the door of the presence of the Lord.

> While the Israelites were camped at Acacia Grove, some of the men defiled themselves by having sexual relations with local Moabite women. . . . When Phinehas son of Eleazar and grandson of Aaron the priest saw this, he jumped up and left the assembly. He took a spear and rushed after the man into his tent. Phinehas thrust the spear all the way through the man's body and into the woman's stomach. So

the plague against the Israelites was stopped, but not before 24,000 people had died.

Numbers 25:1–9 NLT

These are doors to nowhere, and they are leading people away from revelation of more.

It has been said that big doors swing on small hinges. Revelation 4 shows us the biggest and most important door: the door to His realm.

> After these things I looked, and behold, a door standing open in heaven. And the first voice which I heard was like a trumpet speaking with me, saying, "Come up here, and I will show you things which must take place after this." Immediately I was in the Spirit; and behold, a throne set in heaven, and One sat on the throne.

Revelation 4:1–2

It is real. One day we will make a final journey through that door, and waiting on the other side will be a realm that few pay much attention to now. They are preoccupied with new hinges and depleted doors. The hinges on the door to His realm lack attention, and the by-product is rusty hinges.

We do not place enough importance on this small piece of hardware. Without hinges, a door cannot open, close, or be in position. While a hinge is not a complicated device, it does deliver the passage through the door to more. The hinge allows the essence of what is on the other side, the eternal realm, to invade this side, the earthly realm.

One meaning of the word *hinge* is "to move." You can interpret or spiritualize this in a couple of ways: We are to

47

move from glory to glory, or we are to contend for a *move* of God. Either way, the result is more of His presence. But if the hinge is rusty there is no movement. So then, religion takes over. It becomes a form of a walk with God without the crucial substance of what is on the other side. We keep right on going without the atmosphere of the Spirit.

For the sake of releasing the authority of the Lord on this earth, we should be gripped by the intense need to keep the hinges of the door to His presence oiled and in working order. Satan recognizes one thing: authority. When the sons of Sceva decided to try to operate without spiritual authority, the demon said to them, "Jesus I know, and Paul I know; but who are you?" (Acts 19:15). This is a gripping indictment against those who do not know how to keep the hinge oiled and the door open to His realm. Without this discipline, we operate without authority. And Satan laughs.

Halted hinges result in dormant doors. Dormant doors are idle with no activity and no movement. This has produced surface, superficial Christians and churches. This leads to an all-important quote from my book *Doorkeepers of Revival*:

> Never forget that revival requires an open door, an access, or an entry point. The entry point is the place of personal and corporate hunger and pursuit of more of God in prayer and personal sacrifice. . . . The bottom line to sustaining revival: doing whatever it takes, no matter how long it takes, to keep the door of revival open. . . . A doorkeeper allows access and entry. . . . A doorkeeper guards the door making certain that revival has an access point. . . . They occupy a position and an assignment and at all costs will not allow the door to go unattended. There is a constant watch at the door making sure that it's open to revival.[2]

The entire thought surrounding this quote has been about the door, but this recent prophetic word now forces us to look at the hinges to the door. This adds yet another layer of responsibility to the doorkeeper. Doorkeepers were Levites stationed at the gates of God's house. It was their task to open the temple gates in the morning and close them again at night.[3] What seems like a trivial task turns out to be a pivotal position!

If the doors go unattended, the hinges become rusty. Anything not used gets rusty. Could it be that in our looking for *prominent positions* we have missed the *pivotal position*? David shows us this pivotal position. "For a day in Your house is better than a thousand outside. I would rather be the one who opens the door of the house of my God, than to live in the tents of the sinful" (Psalm 84:10 NLV). I also like how *The Passion Translation* handles this passage:

> For just one day of intimacy with you is like a
>   thousand days of joy rolled into one!
> I'd rather stand at the threshold in front of the Gate
>   Beautiful,
> ready to go in and worship my God,
> than to live my life without you
> in the most beautiful palace of the wicked.
>
> Psalm 84:10 TPT

The psalmist says there is no other responsibility that is more important than the position of swinging the door to His presence. Yet the priority of the modern Church seems to be selfish. They want to be a prophet. They want to travel and put up tents. They want to be an apostle. They want to be a preacher.

These are all valuable, biblical, and necessary, but they leave out the valuable position of doorkeeper. Who wants to be the one that keeps the hinges oiled? Somebody must be aware of the rusty hinges on the doors to His realm that have been idle and dormant. We've left our post at the door to more and are reaping the consequences of depleted spirits and deficits of spiritual authority.

If the doors go unattended, the hinges become rusty.

There is always more to be gained from His presence, so someone must stay at the door. I exhort you never to forget the power of that hinge. It opens doors to His presence, and only a doorkeeper will care about that important point. Because only a doorkeeper is responsible for what is on the other side of that door.

And that presents another problem. We've lost sight of the responsibility of keeping the door because we have so many crutches that can keep us going with a closed door and a rusty hinge. May we have a renewed revelation and sense of responsibility to watch over the door and oil the hinges. It comes with a revelation of more. David's tent had two doorkeepers, and he provided four thousand doorkeepers for the new temple that Solomon would build. This shows us the value of a doorkeeper and how it is a pivotal position.

The doors to nowhere have run their course. There is spiritual hunger that cannot be satisfied. Those who have been led through these doors are looking for the way into more, and there's only one who can open it for them—a doorkeeper who has oiled the hinge and stands ready at the door to more.

Perhaps you are one of those who has walked through a door to nowhere and you feel empty and unsatisfied. I have good news. You can be a doorkeeper. Take your position at the door to His presence and begin to do what it takes to get oil for those hinges. God is faithful to lead you into His more. The next room is waiting for you—swing that door today.

Let's talk about fresh oil. The reason for rusty hinges is due to *the cost* of the oil. Oil is a type of the Holy Spirit, and the cost to get this anointing for access to more is great. Doors to His presence sit dormant due to a lack of spiritual discipline and understanding of the cost of the oil. It is not that God is trying to make it difficult to access His realm—it is actually quite easy because of the blood of Jesus Christ—but our flesh will repel any sacrifice and inconvenience that is required. As well, Satan will make sure that you have a convenient substitute that will make you feel satisfied but will include a spiritual deficit. He did this with Eve in the Garden of Eden.

This is why I am talking about the cost of the oil. Success in your spiritual pursuit requires a constant sacrifice of your flesh, your soulish man. This is not a word that we hear much about, yet it is from cover to cover in the Word of God in one form or another. If you take sacrifice out of the Bible, you will not have much left. It is futile to think that we are going to get around this vital principle of sacrifice, especially in our spiritual pursuit. With this said, let us look at some examples of those who paid the price for the oil. Just ask the widow woman about the cost of the oil.

One day the widow of a member of the group of prophets came to Elisha and cried out, "My husband who served you is dead, and you know how he feared the LORD. But now a creditor has come, threatening to take my two sons as

51

slaves." "What can I do to help you?" Elisha asked. "Tell me, what do you have in the house?" "Nothing at all, except a flask of olive oil," she replied. And Elisha said, "Borrow as many empty jars as you can from your friends and neighbors. Then go into your house with your sons and shut the door behind you. Pour olive oil from your flask into the jars, setting each one aside when it is filled." So she did as she was told. Her sons kept bringing jars to her, and she filled one after another. Soon every container was full to the brim!

2 Kings 4:1–6 NLT

She had no husband, she was in debt, and the creditors were coming for her sons. It was a horrible situation to be in, especially for a woman. She was called upon by the prophet to do an illogical, irrational thing: Give God what little you have so that He can make it more. This is the cost of the oil.

Possibly you have been so busy holding onto your small portion of pursuit that you've lost the oil. You have failed to understand that sowing more of yourself gets you more of Him! I do not say that to demean where you are in your spiritual pursuit. I say it to prayerfully cause you to consider that paying a higher cost will open a door to more.

It cannot go unnoticed that the widow was specifically told to shut the door behind her and her sons. This reminds me of another time already mentioned in the previous chapter where we're told to shut the door. "But you, when you pray, go into your inner room, close your door and pray to your Father who is in secret, and your Father who sees what is done in secret will reward you" (Matthew 6:6 NASB).

I have been talking about open doors, but we cannot effectively open doors until we have shut the door behind us to pray. This is the cost of the oil. We try to find too many shortcuts that involve the least amount of effort. It cost this widow everything she had. She had to risk what she was holding to behold the supernatural. This is the cost of the oil.

Just ask the woman with the alabaster box about the cost of the oil.

> Now when Jesus was in Bethany, at the home of Simon the leper, a woman came to Him with an alabaster vial of very costly perfume, and she poured it on His head as He reclined at the table. But the disciples were indignant when they saw this, and said, "Why this waste? For this perfume might have been sold for a high price and the money given to the poor." But Jesus, aware of this, said to them, "Why do you bother the woman? For she has done a good deed to Me. For you always have the poor with you; but you do not always have Me. For when she poured this perfume on My body, she did it to prepare Me for burial. Truly I say to you, wherever this gospel is preached in the whole world, what this woman has done will also be spoken of in memory of her."
>
> Matthew 26:6–13 NASB

This box of perfume cost an entire year's wage. Do the math with your income. Even in the context of money, are you willing to pay the cost for the oil? Don't misunderstand—the blood of Jesus has given us free access in the Spirit; however, in the natural, our sacrificial seeds sown are a memorial to the Lord (see Acts 10:1–4). It is a part of your pursuit, and it is a vital principle that unlocks the door to more. Does this mean it will unlock more money? Possibly. But even greater than currency, it can unlock blessing and a path to the realm where lack doesn't exist. We struggle with ten percent, yet this woman gave an entire year's wage. She didn't think about the cost because her passion was driving her pursuit for more.

Too often, our lack of desire fuels our lack of generosity, which is another reason we have rusty hinges on the door to more. Generosity is a powerful principle in our pursuit of Him. Ask the Holy Spirit to give you a greater desire to sow for more. The disciples in the house wanted to sell the perfume for a profit. They had a scheduled meeting with Jesus, yet still did not understand the price of the oil. Generosity will be a test in your spiritual pursuit, as it was for Ananias and Saphira, as you consider the cost of the oil.

Another powerful aspect within this woman's sacrifice was that she interrupted what I like to call a men's small group with Jesus. He was their special guest. Possibly, they had spent hours planning and preparing for Jesus to come. If we can put it in the context of our day, they had advertised, cooked, cleaned, and carved out a special program just for Jesus. Here they had His captive attention, ready to take selfies with Him to post to their social media accounts, when suddenly a desperate woman in pursuit of the King rushes in and disturbs their plans. They were indignant, annoyed, disgruntled, offended, upset, and disturbed. At this point, her reputation—and possibly her life—was at risk. Still, that truth did not deter her from her pursuit of more. The cost of her reputation seemingly didn't faze her. She threw herself at Jesus' feet and began to worship.

Are you willing to risk your reputation with "the small group" to get the oil needed to keep the door swinging? She became a doorkeeper, and Jesus tells us that when the Gospel is preached, she will be mentioned because she knew the cost of the oil.

Just ask the wise and foolish virgins the cost of the oil.

"Then the kingdom of heaven shall be likened to ten virgins who took their lamps and went out to meet the bridegroom. Now five of them were wise, and five were foolish. Those who were foolish took their lamps and took no oil with them, but the wise took oil in their vessels with their lamps. But while the bridegroom was delayed, they all slumbered and slept. And at midnight a cry was heard: 'Behold, the bridegroom is coming; go out to meet him!' Then all those virgins arose and trimmed their lamps. And the foolish said to the wise, 'Give us some of your oil, for our lamps are going out.' But the wise answered, saying, 'No, lest there should not be enough for us and you; but go rather to those who sell, and buy for yourselves.' And while they went to buy, the bridegroom came, and those who were ready went in with him to the wedding; and the door was shut."

Matthew 25:1–10

Weddings required guests carrying lamps and wicks as opposed to flowers as they awaited the bridegroom.

The ten virgins may be bridesmaids who have been assisting the bride; and they expect to meet the groom as he comes from the bride's house. . . . Everyone in the procession was expected to carry his or her own torch. Those without a torch would be assumed to be party crashers or even brigands. The festivities, which might last several days, would formally get under way at the groom's house.[4]

The torch was either a lamp with a small oil tank and wick or a stick with a rag soaked in oil on the end of it which would require occasional re-soaking to maintain the flame.[5]

Did you notice the last few words of that commentary? "An occasional re-soaking to maintain the flame"! First of all, you had to have a torch to be at the wedding, and second of all, you were responsible for bringing enough oil to keep the flame burning until you saw the bridegroom. What a sacrifice and a responsibility due to the cost of the oil. The flame or passion of your pursuit would be snuffed out if you didn't understand the cost of the oil. Prepare to have enough oil to linger until you see Him!

The unwise, however, didn't have enough oil to last throughout the night to access the door to see the bridegroom. We are not told why they planned poorly, but we can guess that they were excited to be invited to the wedding, but they didn't possess enough passion to pay the price of the oil to actually see the bridegroom. This is an immensely powerful and gripping thought. How often do we stop short due to the cost of the oil? We get so far into the wedding but fail to realize that the cost is greater than we want to pay; therefore, we miss our entry into more.

The wise virgins were not thrown by the poor planning on the part of the unwise. It did not constitute an emergency for them. They simply told the unprepared virgins to go buy their own oil. That is a sermon that many have preached. As you are on your own pursuit of revival, remember that the hinges that swung for the great revivals of old were oiled by ordinary people who understood the cost of the oil. These revivalists unlocked realms of glory and supernatural gifts from the inner court of heaven that touched not only them but also nations. We read and preach about them and pray

Prepare to have enough oil to linger until you see Him!

to taste what they had, but we cannot use their oil. We must buy our own. This is the cost of the oil.

We must not be like the five foolish virgins who are happy to get invited to the party, but who, in their excitement about the temporal, don't think about paying the price to get oil to see the bridegroom, which is what the wedding is all about. And when they went to buy oil, the *door was shut*. We know this is referring to the end times, but we can also think about it as the spiritual door that we've been referring to in this chapter. We never want to arrive at the place where Jesus has to shut the door. He is giving us ample time to access oil. The hinges are rusty—pay whatever it costs for the oil.

Ask Esther about the cost of the oil. Esther had six months of *oil treatment* before the door to the king opened (see Esther 2:12). Impatience in the wait on our spiritual pursuit has resulted in rusty hinges on the doors of glory. We must wait at the gate. "Blessed is the man who listens to me, watching daily at my gates, waiting at the posts of my doors" (Proverbs 8:34).

Much has been said about waiting in the presence of the Lord. But when it comes to getting the oil, waiting is the most important aspect of the cost. There is something about lingering in glory. It is difficult to articulate, but once you have done so and realize the outcome of the wait is that you are saturated in the oil, you will find yourself returning again and again. The amount of time you spend will be outweighed by the amount of oil you receive. There is really no comparison. After a while, waiting won't seem like a sacrifice. The joy of being with Jesus, of becoming like Jesus, and of carrying what Jesus carries far exceeds any amount of time that you will have given.

Hannah, the Syrophoenician woman, the woman, and the unjust judge, would not relent (see 1 Samuel 1; Mark 7:24–30; Luke 18:1–8). We want open doors and well-oiled hinges but say we do not have time. We are available for anything that we really desire. Do we desire doors that swing to the supernatural? Are we desperate for what is beyond the door? Do the time and count the cost of the oil. "Keep on asking and it will be given you; keep on seeking and you will find; keep on knocking [reverently] and [the door] will be opened to you" (Matthew 7:7 AMPC).

And finally, just ask the servant the cost of the oil. "Make this servant put his ear against your door and use a sharp tool to make a hole in his ear. This will show that he is your slave forever" (Deuteronomy 15:17 ERV). In this story, the door is the object used to prove our loyalty, faithfulness, and the commitment. It is what shows that our dedication is permanent. This is the cost of the oil.

We are available for anything that we really desire.

We get excited about visitations of the Lord, as we should, but the cost of the oil for habitation is entirely different than the cost for just an occasional encounter. If you want Him to stay, you must stay. The issue has never been will He stay, but will you stay? Habitation is the place where you live in personal revival. This is the ultimate desire and intention of God and why He sent Jesus Christ. He opened a way for us to access Him 24/7. Just one call and He is there. I often say, He's on the other side of your cry. He's waiting to manifest, but it takes our commitment to *stay* in pursuit. This leads me to one who stayed and paid the price for the oil.

Moses took his tent and pitched it outside the camp, far from the camp, and called it the tabernacle of meeting. And it came to pass that everyone who sought the LORD went out to the tabernacle of meeting which was outside the camp. So it was, whenever Moses went out to the tabernacle, that all the people rose, and each man stood at his tent door and watched Moses until he had gone into the tabernacle. And it came to pass, when Moses entered the tabernacle, that the pillar of cloud descended and stood at the door of the tabernacle, and the LORD talked with Moses. All the people saw the pillar of cloud standing at the tabernacle door, and all the people rose and worshiped, each man in his tent door. So the LORD spoke to Moses face to face, as a man speaks to his friend. And he would return to the camp, but his servant Joshua the son of Nun, a young man, did not depart from the tabernacle.

Exodus 33:7–11

Did you notice that his helper, Joshua son of Nun, always stayed in the tent? Just as the servant who pierced his ear to the door to prove his permanent service, Joshua stayed behind the door and tarried in the tent proving his permanent worship and loyalty to God's call. Sometimes when you spiritually get beyond that door, lingering and tarrying must also transpire to accomplish the purpose of the Lord on this side of the door. There is oil, Joshua, that you need to lead a nation that you will not find in any other place than tarrying in the tent behind the door. This is the cost of the oil.

As I close this chapter on the revelation of more, I need to show you one more insight: the cost of holiness and purity. Living a life of holiness is a choice. It is a personal choice to walk separated unto the Lord and worthy of the Gospel by obeying and honoring His commands and the principles of His Word. Those who cultivate desperation in their lives will make holiness and purity a priority. The Bible says that without it we will not see God (see Hebrews 12:14) and only the pure in heart will see Him (see Matthew 5:8).

How can you stay desperate for someone that you never see? In all we do, we want to please Him so that we will always see Him. This is the heart of the desperate and leads us to focus on the hinges of the door. "Thus Solomon had all the furnishings made for the house of the LORD . . . the hinges of gold, both for the doors of the inner room (the Most Holy Place)" (1 Kings 7:48–50). Notice that the hinges on the door to glory were made of gold. Many things that surrounded the temple worship courts were made of gold for the reason of purity. Gold contains no mixture, it is pure. Jesus told the lukewarm church, "I advise you to buy from Me gold refined by fire" (Revelation 3:18 NASB).

And this is required of us as well.

> Who may ascend into the hill of the LORD?
> Or who may stand in His holy place?
> He who has clean hands and a pure heart,
> Who has not lifted up his soul to an idol,
> Nor sworn deceitfully.
> He shall receive blessing from the LORD,
> And righteousness from the God of his salvation.
> Psalm 24:3–5

Rusty hinges! Rusty hinges! They have been locked down for decades. Those who are committed to pay the cost for the oil and permanently attend the door understand that their service begins with a pure heart and clean hands. Then, a transfer happens—those rusty hinges somehow become gold or pure. Those who linger and stand close to the Most Holy place understand that this door swings on pure hinges. The longer you linger, the purer you become. You cannot stay close to Him and remain impure. You will either leave or learn to be holy.

I invite you into the revelation of more. I invite you to make a commitment to be a doorkeeper of revival in your life. Make sure that daily you have oil for the hinges that swing on the door to more referred to in Revelation 4. Do not flinch at the sacrifice. It is a commitment to do whatever it takes, and it is worth it all. The revelation of more. There is another room waiting for your pursuit. Don't stop, don't stall. Keep walking. Stay desperate. There is always more.

FOUR

The Eternal Pull— the Case for Personal Revival

Remember, revival is the transformation of a life from spiritual dryness to spiritual zeal and passion for the Lord. In the last chapter, I mentioned that we should have an eternal perspective concerning our spiritual pursuit. My experience has been that when believers do not understand the eternal scope of revival, they will stall or end their pursuit. It is my hope that this chapter will inspire you toward that goal. I hope it will challenge you and change your entire outlook on your time with God.

When you pull away into your secret place to begin walking with God into the rooms of more, realize that you are answering a divine call that has been placed within every human heart. Not all respond, but those who do realize it was more than a decision of the mind—it was a response to a pull within called *eternity*. Along our pursuit, we must never forget to defer to the pull of eternity. Two key verses point us to this pull:

> For everything there is a season, a time for every activity under heaven. . . . Yet God has made everything beautiful for its own time. He has planted eternity in the human heart.
>
> Ecclesiastes 3:1, 11 NLT

> While we look not at the things which are seen, but at the things which are not seen; for the things which are seen are temporal, but the things which are not seen are eternal.
>
> 2 Corinthians 4:18 NASB

You can try to ignore it, but it is divinely implanted. You may try to explain it away (as many so-called atheists have tried), but it is there. Eternity is in your heart. The deepest part of who you are has an eternal stamp upon it. What you do with it is a determination of your will. God lets you choose, but the pull is always there. You will never get away from it. Never. There are many things we can control in this life and this world, but eternity is not one of them. No matter what you do, where you go, or who you are, eternity is in your heart. The eternal pull is always there.

Along our pursuit, we must never forget to defer to the pull of eternity.

To pull is to draw with force. Eternity being in our heart means there is an ever-present eternal longing. God has divinely placed an eternal, forever longing within the deepest part of who we are. The place that we have no ability to alter on our own contains a never-ending longing for Him. His presence. His realm. Him alone. This awareness will live forever, an eternal pulse that cannot be stopped. Because of this divine placement of eternity, you will always have awareness that there is more; therefore, you will always have a longing for personal revival, for a life full of intense spiritual zeal, and for endless passion for the Lord.

Revival is simply the return to awareness of what and who you were made for. We are made to worship God, and we are made for His pleasure. Anything that takes your attention or allegiance from this is an idol and has caused you to compromise your position and eternal purpose. When you are in that state, you need personal revival, the return to intense spiritual zeal and passion for the Lord.

No matter what you achieve or the goals you reach, you will always find that there is something missing because there is an eternal pull toward more. Revival, as I believe and have experienced, is the return to the eternal hunger for the more that pulsates within.

The only hope that Satan has is to try to dull, slow, or deafen that eternal pulse beat by amplifying the temporal. The god of this world and the spirit of the age will grip our souls creating a soul tie—a superglue bonding to the things of the world. You may have wondered how people can revert to carnality and the attractions of the world. The answer is, they did not cut the tie to the temporal.

The grace of God has placed within us a pull to more, but the more we ignore the pull, the farther we drift away from our pursuit. Do not ignore the pull. Each season of life can be enjoyed but will never truly satisfy. In the end, we must fear God and keep His commandments for this is man's all (see Ecclesiastes 12:13). This world is not our home. We must cut the tie.

If we find ourselves with a desire that nothing in this world can satisfy, the most probable explanation is that we were made for another world.

C. S. Lewis, *Mere Christianity*[1]

We were made for another world. We were made for more. You can resist the pull, but resistance results in a miserable, unfulfilled life and a dark eternity. Personal revival demands our full attention because revival is the return to more. You cannot walk into more while holding on to or being chained to the lesser. There is a constant tug-o-war in the inward man. The tug of the temporal versus the pull of the eternal. The one that wins is the one to which we defer.

We are continually being forced to make decisions concerning these two choices. The way we respond, or react to each of these, will greatly affect our spiritual growth and development.

Spiritual things are desirable only to those who have been born of the Spirit and are spiritually minded. Therefore, with a higher purpose in view, the Lord made the "*tree of life*" very ordinary, and the "*tree of the knowledge of good and evil*" very attractive.

The tree of life, which is the person of the Lord Jesus Christ, appears to us as being "*a root out of a dry ground, having no form nor comeliness and when we see Him, there is no outward beauty that we should desire or choose Him*" (Isaiah 53:2).

The tree of the knowledge of good and evil is quite different. It appears as being "*good for food, pleasant to the eye, and one to be desired*" (Genesis 3:6). It appeals to every aspect of our flesh life. Thus, on the surface, a temporal self-centered life appears to be very attractive. However, this is deceptive as it will pass away in a moment. It offers no true inner satisfaction or eternal reward.[2]

This is a powerful quote and a perfect illustration for the pull versus the tug. Which tree are you drawn to? That is the tree you are feeding the most and the realm to which you are connected. I trust that you are seeing the investment in your pursuit. It will not be flashy, but it will be fulfilling. Jesus came to bring us fulfillment. Even those who followed Him during His time on earth wanted flashy, they wanted a king to rescue them from Roman tyranny. But Jesus came for a much greater purpose. He didn't come to give them temporal relief—He wanted them to have eternal rest.

For us to see revival flourish, we must cut ties with the temporal. The pressure of revival pulls against the pressure of the temporal and flesh. It will always be that way. Revival will not befriend your flesh or carnality. If it does, it is not revival. The only thing strong enough to break the pressure of the temporal is the pressure of His presence. This is revival. All else in this world is inferior to His presence. His presence must increase in your heart to break the tie of the temporal. When you are touched by that realm, you will see that this realm is of little significance to you.

You may reply, "I don't want to be so heavenly minded that I'm no earthly good." You will never be any earthly good until you are heavenly minded. You will never be able to help anyone on this earth for good because your good will always fall short of what they truly need. They are looking

His presence must increase in your heart to break the tie of the temporal.

for someone who can help them defer to the pull. If you defend carnality, you reveal that His presence is not the primary atmosphere of your life because you cannot live in close proximity to His presence and desire a lesser pursuit.

The devil has placed chains around good people to lure them to hell. These chains are not always wicked or perverse. They are simply chains to the temporal that keep people tied down so that they cannot ascend with the divine pull. And then they will stay linked to a worldly cosmos (influence of the temporal). Before they know it, their passion is gone, their spiritual longing has waned, their fervency has diminished, and their spiritual pursuit has been hijacked. They need revival. This is the case for personal revival.

At this point, the only pressure that can break the grip of the temporal is the pressure of His presence that makes the hills melt like wax and makes the mountains shake. This is why we must defer to the pull so the temporal that has captivated us will shake and melt. It is the only answer to the resistance of the eternal pull.

You see, once you have tasted it, you cannot return to nominal. If you're feeling uncomfortable, and possibly a bit angry at the challenge, then I have done my job. My goal is to allow you to see that there's something stronger than you think holding you down and something greater than you imagine that is trying to pull you higher. If no one ever tells you there is more, you will meander in the lesser and live way below the pulse beat within that's pulling you toward more.

The case for revival? If you can honestly say that you want the temporal to win the tug-o-war, you have settled, and this is not what Jesus intended. It is exceedingly difficult to reach someone whose thought processes and flesh are bound by Satan and the temporal. Until that chain is broken, you will feel the pressure of the tug of that chain that keeps you connected and earthbound.

Take a step away from this earth, time, and all that you know. Look at your eternal choices: heaven or hell. Nothing that you choose right now that ranks higher than personal spiritual pursuit, revival, and the return to who and what you were made for, will benefit that day. Nothing. The apostle Paul gives us a precise directive to counter any temptation to the temporal.

> If then you were raised with Christ, seek those things which are above, where Christ is, sitting at the right hand of God. Set your mind on things above, not on things on the earth. For you died, and your life is hidden with Christ in God. When Christ who is our life appears, then you also will appear with Him in glory. Therefore put to death your members which are on the earth: fornication, uncleanness, passion, evil desire, and covetousness, which is idolatry.
>
> Colossians 3:1–5

Seek the things above and set your mind on those things. Put to death the things of the flesh. This is how you cut the tie to the temporal. As you do this, your sensitivity to the Spirit will increase. You will have once again amplified the pulse beat of eternity within. What was once covered with the sounds of the world and the spirit of the age is now clear and distinct. The sounds of eternity are ruling in your heart as God always intended for them to do.

> There is a natural body, and there is a spiritual body. And so it is written, "The first man Adam became a living being." The

69

last Adam became a life-giving spirit. However, the spiritual is not first, but the natural, and afterward the spiritual. The first man was of the earth, made of dust; the second Man is the Lord from heaven. As was the man of dust, so also are those who are made of dust; and as is the heavenly Man, so also are those who are heavenly. And as we have borne the image of the man of dust, we shall also bear the image of the heavenly Man.

1 Corinthians 15:44–49

This verse is a clear picture that we are made for more. In His grace, God has given us this natural body. But within us is the spiritual man pulsating with the rhythm of the eternal throne. The more you try to tie the spirit man down, the weaker it gets. While you feed the flesh, the eternal longing starves for its eternal home.

If you are making righteous choices, your spirit becomes more sensitive and responsive to His presence. But if you are living for carnal gratification—and when I say living for, I mean that is your happiness and pursuit—then it will not be very long before you're hardened and indifferent to the Lord and His presence. Small things matter when eternal things are being pursued. This is a huge statement for those who prioritize their spiritual pursuit.

This is way more than only about right or wrong. Those values are vital, but the higher purpose is to partake of the Spirit and life. There is a high price of the flesh, but if the price is paid, you live on a higher plain of spirituality. And the place at which you end is the place where you begin in the next. "Behold, I stand at the door and knock; if anyone hears My voice and opens the door, I will come in to him and will dine with him, and he with Me" (Revelation 3:20 NASB).

This is the same door as in Revelation 4 and is where the pull originates. It is the location of the entrance to your heart. Only you can answer the knock. He is pulling, and He is knocking. Jesus will come in and dine with us, the Bible says, and the feast we share is revival. This is what the pursuit is all about. But only you can answer the knock.

To be given something eternal and not host it, steward it, and nurture it is like the irresponsible, lazy, and even wicked servant (see Matthew 25:14–30). In His grace and mercy, however, He has given us conviction. If we humble ourselves, die to our flesh, and defer to the pull, we will open the door to the pull of eternity.

Small things matter when eternal things are being pursued.

Conviction is like a check engine light in our automobiles. When the light is illuminated, we know we need to check below the surface of what we can see. We need to investigate what is causing the malfunction, dysfunction, or damage. One of the reasons that people do not cut the ties to the temporal is because they have allowed the voice of conviction to be silenced. When conviction is silenced, carnality will rule.

Conviction is a feeling from the Holy Spirit that accompanies a compromised belief or principle. "When He arrives, He will uncover [convict] the sins of the world, expose unbelief as sin, and allow all to see their sins in the light of righteousness for the first time" (John 16:8–9 THE VOICE).

Conviction is a protection in our lives—condemnation is a penalty of religion. We must learn to respect and honor the conviction of the Holy Spirit who empowers our spiritual pursuit. When Jesus encountered the woman caught in adultery, He told her that He did not condemn her and that she was to go her way and sin no more (see John 18:11). Please note that Jesus did not leave her at, "Go your way." He moved her into, "Sin no more." True conviction will always lead you into sin no more. A modern rendition of this verse would stop at go your way, but a repentant heart will follow Holy Spirit conviction into sin no more.

We do not want to be like the Laodicean church who did not realize they were poor, naked, and blind (see Revelation 3:17). They refused the voice of conviction and were therefore blinded to their deficit. If we ignore the voice of conviction too long, our conscience will become immune to the sound. The Lord told the Laodiceans to be shamelessly committed to Him. Only when we are shamelessly committed will we be truly rich, see clearly, and have our shame covered.

You cannot live wrong and die right. Trends have deceived people to thinking they can live as the world does and still be holy. One day, they will wake up on the wrong side of that trend, regretting that they ignored the pull and chose the tug.

The voice of conviction leads you upward, toward the eternal. Defer to this pull. Your address is in this world, but your home is in eternity. Never forget that you will always feel the eternal pull. Personal revival is the return to the eternal hunger that is innate within each of us as human beings. It is forever pulsating. Eternity is in your heart pulling you toward more. Do you hear the rhythm of His realm? Defer to that pull!

FIVE

Joined to the Lord

As we cut ties to the temporal and defer to the eternal pull, we must be very intentional in our spiritual pursuit to be joined to the Lord. To be joined to the Lord means that we are vitally united in an intimate relationship. It is possible to be joined, loyal, and in covenant with another lover. One of the primary titles and roles we have as the Church is to be a Bride, the Bride of Christ.

Obviously, the relationship dynamics are a mirror and parallel to an earthly marriage between husband and wife. Jesus is our Bridegroom, and our relationship with Him should mirror the intimacy of a husband and wife, bride and bridegroom. The level of implied intimacy with this title and role is clear. Covenant brings closeness and closeness keeps covenant. To demonstrate this nonnegotiable principle of being united to the Lord, we can look at a few Bible passages.

> For I am zealous for you with a godly eagerness and a divine jealousy, for I have betrothed you to one Husband, to

present you as a chaste [pure, undefiled] virgin to Christ. But [now] I am fearful, lest that even as the serpent beguiled Eve by his cunning, so your minds may be corrupted and seduced from wholehearted and sincere and pure devotion to Christ.

2 Corinthians 11:2–3 AMPC

And I will betroth you to Me forever; yes, I will betroth you to Me in righteousness and justice, in steadfast love, and in mercy. I will even betroth you to Me in stability and in faithfulness, and you shall know (recognize, be acquainted with, appreciate, give heed to, and cherish) the Lord.

Hosea 2:19–20 AMPC

But he who is joined to the Lord is one spirit with Him.

1 Corinthians 6:17

The following is a dream that I had that demonstrates the relationship dynamics of being joined to the Lord.

I was alone and traveling, via GPS, to a wedding in a mountaintop area. When I arrived, I found myself in a relatively small room where none of the guests of the wedding were familiar to me.

About that time, I noticed the bride, someone who was very familiar to me; however, in the dream, she was marrying a man who was not her real-life husband. I did not recognize the guy/groom she had chosen to marry. I was distraught because I knew she was marrying the wrong man.

After the ceremony she, the new groom, and others I didn't recognize were standing outside. It was obvious in the dream that I was part of the family of the bride, but I went to greet the new groom. He was very cold and hesitant to embrace me. I don't remember hearing his name.

When the new groom left the bride's side, I began aggressively pulling her to the side to get her to explain why she had chosen the wrong groom over the correct one. My emotions in the dream were very intense. I grabbed the bride, saying, "Why didn't you tell us?" She never really gave an answer.

I then noticed someone in the wedding party waiting on her, and realized it was the man she should've married. He didn't speak, but I felt his deep disappointment as he left.

I peppered her with questions, pleading for her to come to her senses. "Who is this guy you married? Do you really know him?" As I asked her questions like those, her demeanor was very cold—almost rebellious. She never answered me. The wedding festivities were still in motion, and I knew I had little time with her to convince her to change her mind.

In the natural, she had kids, so in my dream, I asked her how the kids took the new marriage. This was the only answer that I remember her giving. She said, "Oh, it was hard." My emotions at this part of the dream were extremely intense, as I believed I was feeling the cost of her compromise. I knew it was affecting not only her but also the next generation.

She eventually left our conversation by getting in a car to continue the wedding celebrations elsewhere. Extremely distraught, I got in my car to leave. As I made my way down the mountain, I made plans to call the correct man to meet with him. As I traveled down the mountain, the dream ends.

It had been quite some time since I had a dream this vivid and intense. I sensed the Lord speaking His heart and a warning through this dream. His heart is intimacy with His

Bride, the Church, His warning is to be aware of the high places of idolatry.

Dreams are like parables. They are not always easy to immediately understand, even disconnected sometimes, but everything has a meaning. We see this validated in the Bible (see Genesis 41:1–36; Daniel 2:24–47). Still, we must be cautious to pray over them and validate them with the Word of God.

Because of the intensity and atmosphere of the dream, I felt that I needed to take this to prayer. Here are what the dream symbols represent:

- the Bride = the Church
- the (wrong) groom = marrying or joining another lover—the wrong bridegroom
- the other (correct) groom = Jesus, the Beloved
- the mountain = high places of compromise
- kids = the future Church and the impact of this generation's compromise
- Me = the role of the Holy Spirit—bringing awareness to compromise

On your spiritual pursuit, you will encounter seasons of drawing and confrontation by the Holy Spirit. In the drawing seasons, the Lord brings you closer to His ways to know Him. These times are crucial to the success of our spiritual pursuit. In the confrontation times, or searching times, we find ourselves caught in the dealings of the Lord. These times are a byproduct of being brought close. They show us who we are and what we need to deal with. An example of this is when Isaiah saw the Lord and immediately cried, "Woe is me" (Isaiah 6:5). It is inevitable. In these wooing and searching seasons, the Lord wants us to deal with any high places in our lives. You cannot live in a place of revival while occupying a high place of compromise.

> High places, very simply, were places of worship on elevated pieces of ground. High places were originally dedicated to idol worship. . . . The Israelites, forever turning away from God, practiced Molech worship and built high places for Baal. Although Solomon built the temple of God in Jerusalem, he later established idolatrous high places for his foreign wives outside of Jerusalem and worshiped with them, causing him the loss of the kingdom.[1]

In the context of our lives, high places are carnal or sinful choices that cause us to become inebriated, intoxicated, or seduced by another lover. The byproduct is the spirit of confusion (disorder, distraction), which always leads to delusion (false belief) unto rebellion and idolatry (disobedience). High places are places of worship. We can worship *anything* by giving it allegiance and priority.

We operate from a perspective of a false belief because of the delusion brought by a wrong choice. We're tainted by the seduction of the high place, so we cannot *see* to make the right choice; therefore, we choose to *marry or be joined* to that which is not the Lord. This is idolatry.

> **You cannot live in a place of revival while occupying a high place of compromise.**

Idolatry is anything that steals allegiance, love, reverence, worship, or loyalty from the Lord. The Israelites had images they would worship instead of God. Regardless of what the Lord did for them, they repeatedly created this pattern (see Exodus 32; Isaiah 2). They would give their loyalty to another lover. For them, it was a hill with a false god and the demands of its worship.

The Lord has made it clear that we are to worship on one hill only. That is the hill of the Lord. The high place of idolatry is not a place to play until you reach a crisis point and decide to climb the hill of the Lord. This was the history of Israel. They would play on the high places of idolatry until judgment came and then begin to call out for mercy and the hill of the Lord.

> Who may ascend into the hill of the LORD?
> And who may stand in His holy place?
> He who has clean hands and a pure heart,
> Who has not lifted up his soul to falsehood
> And has not sworn deceitfully.
> He shall receive a blessing from the LORD
> And righteousness from the God of his salvation.
> This is the generation of those who seek Him,
> Who seek Your face—even Jacob. Selah.
>
> Psalm 24:3–6 NASB

An elevated God dwells in elevated places. He is high and holy. He dwells in this high and holy place, yet He also dwells with the lowly and contrite *of heart*. To climb the hill of the Lord, you must possess clean hands and a pure heart. Everything points back to the heart, and everything points back to clean and pure. I have often said that we're not required to be perfect because that is not attainable, but we are required to be pure. Pure is without mixture. Pure is without blemish and compromise. In Christ, we can have this posture. We must, however, live a life of daily spiritual examination and re-pentance before the Lord, examining our hearts. "So above all, guard the affections of your heart, for they affect all that you are. Pay attention to the welfare of your innermost being, for from there flows the wellspring of life" (Proverbs 4:23 TPT).

> To climb the hill of the Lord, you must possess clean hands and a pure heart.

The things that we allow to get into our heart affect everything we do. Our attitudes, decisions, and thought processes. If left unguarded, we will find ourselves on the wrong hill, the high place of compromise. At this point, seduction is transferred. It lures us away from our loyalty and the covenants we've made. The pull of seduction leads us to join the wrong lover, which leads to idolatry. This is exactly what I witnessed in my dream.

We must prioritize ascending the hill of the Lord. It is an intentional climb to be joined to Him and Him alone, a holy, tenacious pursuit of God ignoring all diversions. We must have a single eye for Him and no other lover. Our goal is intimacy with the One who dwells on that holy hill. We will go to great lengths to purify and cleanse our heart knowing that as we do, we will collide with His glory at the top of His holy hill.

Please hear the heart of the Lord—we must look at the operation of the Holy Spirit (represented in this dream) as mercy. Once again, revisiting the powerful operation of conviction, the Bible says that He came to convict the world of sin. "And when He comes, He will convict and convince the world and bring demonstration to it about sin and about righteousness (uprightness of heart and

79

right standing with God) and about judgment" (John 16:8 AMPC).

He does not condemn you; He convicts you. Big difference. Condemnation leaves you without hope and no way out, while conviction brings hope and the cross of Christ to show you the way out. Do not miss His warnings and die on the wrong hill. You must heed the promptings, the leadings, pleadings, and the nudges of the love of the Holy Spirit. This is why you must stay close to Him. Anything that the Spirit does to draw your attention to disobedience or compromise is an act of mercy in this time of betrothal.

And that is the primary point of this chapter, we are in a time of betrothal to get ourselves ready as a Bride, the Bride of Christ. Time is short, so the enemy is working to deceive into delusion with the goal of rebellion. So I want to sound an alarm today and say as Paul said, "I am jealous for you with godly jealousy. For I have betrothed you to one husband, that I may present you as a chaste virgin to Christ" (2 Corinthians 11:2).

> This part of Scripture [2 Corinthians 11] is paralleled in the traditional Jewish betrothal and marriage of that time. The man or families would choose the bride. The bridegroom or his family would pay the bride price. Then . . . he would go to his father's house and build on more living space in preparation for his new wife. When the father deemed that it was ready, the son would go for his wife and the wedding celebration would begin. After the celebration and supper, they would go to live in the new building he had constructed at his father's house.[2]

An exact representation of Jesus' blood paid the price for us His Bride, and He went away to prepare a place for us in His Father's house. No man knows the time that the Bridegroom will come except the Father; however, He will soon return to take His Bride to the marriage supper of the Lamb in New Jerusalem. We are in the time of betrothal. As we see in the book of Revelation, we must make ourselves ready. "Blessed (happy, to be envied) are those who are summoned (invited, called) to the marriage supper of the Lamb" (Revelation 19:9 AMPC). And we also read, "Let us rejoice and shout for joy . . . for the marriage of the Lamb [at last] has come, and His bride has prepared herself" (Revelation 19:7 AMPC).

Between our salvation now and the return of Christ then, there are mountains of worship that will be placed before us.

> We are in a time of betrothal to get ourselves ready as a Bride, the Bride of Christ.

We must make the right choices on our spiritual revival pursuit because our high place is where our covenant is made. Our covenant is that to which we are joined, married, and united in our soul. Our soul is our mind, will, and emotions.

Covenant is strong. It is deeper than a word or piece of paper, and it touches the core of who we are. When covenant is broken, we experience tearing away at the deepest part of who we are. In the case of our relationship with the Lord, covenant breaking with Him breaks His heart.

Have you ever thought about divorcing the Lord? Our immediate answer would probably be no; however, our soulish choices that cause us to climb the wrong hill divorce us from our covenant with God. Any hill in our life that compromises or steals our covenant with the Lord is how we divorce Him.

81

Once you are on the wrong hill, you enter an atmosphere of lawlessness and iniquity, and the love for God and people is very cold, just like I saw on the bride's face in the dream. How do I know I am on the wrong hill?

> Do we compromise on the clear commands of God? Do we substitute our thoughts for His truth? Do we choose comfort or convenience, or justify giving into our fleshly desires, rather than committing to full obedience, even if it is costly, uncomfortable, or illogical to our human reasoning? And worse, do we do all this while proclaiming the name of Jesus?[3]

The Bible says that it is because of lawlessness that love will grow cold. "And the love of the great body of people will grow cold because of the multiplied lawlessness and iniquity" (Matthew 24:12 AMPC). The love that grows cold is toward God and each other. A cold love will leave covenant for another lover.

As I faced the bride in my dream, I (the Holy Spirit) was intensely pleading with her with the kind of desperation you feel when everything is completely out of your control, yet you know that it is wrong, and everything within you is trying to persuade a change of heart. James gives a great warning concerning this.

> You [are like] unfaithful wives [having illicit love affairs with the world and breaking your marriage vow to God]! Do you not know that being the world's friend is being God's enemy? So whoever chooses to be a friend of the world takes his stand as an enemy of God. Or do you suppose that the Scripture is speaking to no purpose that says, The Spirit Whom He

has caused to dwell in us yearns over us and He yearns for the Spirit [to be welcome] with a jealous love?

James 4:4–5 AMPC

The Spirit has an all-consuming and passionate desire to have more and more of us. In fact, this desire to possess us is so strong that He literally yearns, craves, and pines after us. . . . Because of this intense desire, He is focused on changing you, empowering you, conforming you to the image of Jesus Christ, and helping you fulfill God's plan for your life. . . . Allow Him to have more and more of you each day. Satisfy the yearning of this Divine Lover. . . . Let Him exercise His authority in your life and flood you with His divine desire![4]

As for the bride in my dream, her response was cold and rebellious. Her response to the deficit she was handing to the next generation was a selfish "Oh, it was hard." The atmosphere of lawlessness had taken over her soul. Lawlessness removes all boundaries of truth, morality, doctrine, conscience, and definition of sin. And while you are playing on that high place, a generation is watching you compromise.

For the sake of an intimate relationship with Jesus, for the sake of the next generation, an intentional season of purity is required from us to remove anything from our lives that contaminates or debases. This is how clear our channels must be so that we recognize and clearly hear our Bridegroom in this season of betrothal. The enemy's warfare will be extremely difficult to discern if we have any mixture of the world in our hearts. If we do not press into purity, we will experience delusion that leads to rebellion. The urgency is resounding in the heavenlies: he who has ear to hear, let him hear!

> You shall utterly destroy all the places where the nations whom you shall dispossess serve their gods, on the high mountains and on the hills and under every green tree. You shall tear down their altars and smash their sacred pillars and burn their Asherim with fire, and you shall cut down the engraved images of their gods and obliterate their name from that place. You shall not act like this toward the LORD your God.
>
> Deuteronomy 12:2–4 NASB

May the Lord put within us the spirit of Josiah to do this. Josiah and Hezekiah were the only two kings who destroyed the high places. Other kings, even if they were good, left the high places. It does make you wonder why they would leave an idolatrous hill of worship knowing that they were commanded to worship only the Lord God. Then again, we should wonder the same thing today.

> Josiah destroyed the high place at Topheth in the Valley of Ben Hinnom. He didn't want anyone to use the high place to sacrifice his son or daughter in the fire to the god named Molek. Josiah removed the statues of horses from the entrance to the LORD's temple. The kings of Judah had set them apart to honor the sun. The statues were in the courtyard. They were near the room of an official named Nathan-Melek. Josiah burned the chariots that had been set apart to honor the sun. He pulled down the altars the kings of Judah had set up. They had put them on the palace roof near the upstairs room of Ahaz. Josiah also pulled down the altars

Manasseh had built. They were in the two courtyards of the
LORD's temple. Josiah removed the altars from there. He
smashed them to pieces. Then he threw the broken pieces
into the Kidron Valley.

2 Kings 23:10–12 NIRV

The heart of Josiah was gripped by revelation of the Word
of God concerning covenant with the Lord. The goal of our
spiritual pursuit is to be married to the Lord on the hill of
the Lord.

The language of intimacy is used to describe the type of
relationship we are to have with Jesus. True revival will always result in a revival of intimacy with Christ. This place of
intimacy is one that must be protected. It will be challenged
on all fronts. We will be seduced by the world, the flesh, and
the devil to give our loyalty and love to another lover, but
if we're joined to the Lord, our resolve will be greater than
the resistance. When we are joined to the Lord, we are one
spirit with Him, and our spirit becomes stronger than the
lure of the high place. "But he who is joined to the Lord is
one spirit with Him" (1 Corinthians 6:17).

To be joined to the Lord means we are vitally united and
connected, and we are abiding in Him. This verse is sand-
wiched between exhortations against sexual sin. Paul's lesson to the Jewish people is that when you join yourself to
a harlot (another lover) you become one with them. This is
where we get the basis for soul ties. It is important to get the
context that the apostle Paul lays out in these verses.

A soul tie can be both emotional and sexual. Either is like
superglue for the soul. You can't shake it on your own. You
are bound beyond your human ability to disconnect. The

sexual sin that Paul was addressing is more than a physical act, it is spiritual, emotional, and mental engagement. Every part of our being begins to take ownership and connection to the other person because God intended the sexual union to tightly unite and bind husband and wife together. This is proved when the Bible says, "What God has joined together, let not man separate" (Matthew 19:6). Have you ever wondered why someone can't separate from the high place? It is because they are joined to it.

True revival will always result in a revival of intimacy with Christ.

With this in mind, we see the strong connotation of the words joined to the Lord that we read earlier in 1 Corinthians 6:17. The intensity of intimacy that God longs for is compared to that of the intimacy of a husband and wife. It is the most intimate example that we have, so we must hear God's heart as He uses the language of marital intimacy to describe the type of relationship He desires with His Bride.

> And I will betroth you to Me forever; yes, I will betroth you to Me in righteousness and justice, in steadfast love, and in mercy. I will even betroth you to Me in stability and in faithfulness, and you shall know (recognize, be acquainted with, appreciate, give heed to, and cherish) the Lord.
>
> Hosea 2:19–20 AMPC

Hosea used a marriage covenant as a symbol of God's covenant with Israel. God had been faithful to His people, but they had broken their vows and chased after other "lovers."[5]

It is unfortunate, but common, that some will date God while joined or married to another on the high place of compromise. Israel did it. They built a golden calf. "And when Aaron saw the molten calf, he built an altar before it; and Aaron made proclamation, and said, Tomorrow shall be a feast to the Lord" (Exodus 32:5 AMPC).

The idol he crafted for them was a calf, but Aaron maintained the name of the Lord in connection with it. They were dating God but married to another! This is the delusion that I speak of, and it is still active today. And remember, while you are playing on that high place, a generation is watching your compromise and hearing you still call it Lord.

To be joined to the Lord is a choice, and it should be the core of your spiritual pursuit. It is where you decide to do that which exposes you to Him and keeps you in contact and covenant with Him.

> "May he kiss me with the kisses of his mouth! For your love is better than wine. Your oils have a pleasing fragrance, your name is like purified oil; therefore the maidens love you. Draw me after you and let us run together! The king has brought me into his chambers. We will rejoice in you and be glad; we will extol your love more than wine. Rightly do they love you."
>
> Song of Solomon 1:1–4 NASB

Much like today, wine in the Bible was a substance that satisfied the soul but not the spirit. The verse says that God's kiss—love and oils, indicative of intimacy—are better than wine. God's kiss or intimacy is more fulfilling and runs deeper than the wine of the world that merely appeases and numbs the senses. The bride in this verse is giving all to her lover (Jesus Christ). There is truly no comparison to the cultivated love of Christ, but until you give it all, you will be tempted and taunted to continue to get your fix with the wine of the world.

Then she cries, "Draw me after you and let us run together!" The commitment to intentional pursuit is seen in these words. "Draw near to God and He will draw near to you" (James 4:8). Run with Him, and the King will bring you into His presence. The language of intimacy requires more than singing words on a screen on Sunday only to leave and climb a high place of compromise on Monday. Our satisfaction must be found in Him alone, and it will be if we cry, "Draw me near to You!" "As for me . . . I will be satisfied with Your likeness when I awake" (Psalm 17:15 NASB).

He is seeking more than your talent and accomplishments. He's seeking your covenant. You can do things for God and still live on a high place of compromise. Spiritual activity can be addictive and can become a high place. It can also make us view God as a boss and us as employees just putting in our time. We clock out and then climb the high place. But the Lord desires a marriage relationship with oneness and unity. Joined to the Lord, united to the Lord. He desires your yielded-ness and commitment to continue in vital union with Him. This was the prayer of Jesus: "That they all may be one, [just] as You, Father, are in Me and I in You, that they also may be one in Us" (John 17:21 AMPC).

So many are trying to work for Him, but He longs for us to be united with Him in an intimate, dependent, covenant relationship. Spiritual maturity and spiritual capacity accelerate when we begin to see Jesus as the Bridegroom who is seeking our attention and affection. "Who is this who comes up from the wilderness leaning upon her beloved?" (Song of Solomon 8:5 AMPC).

This is a picture of the bride leaning on her beloved, and it is a beautiful picture of complete surrender and dependence on Him. It shows us how we are close and at one with Him. Anything else that tried to compete is not the one we choose—He is our choice. The bride has come out of the wilderness, and we can speak of those times of drawing and confrontation that we began with in this chapter. The bride comes to the end of her abilities and confesses her need of Him. It is here that we see her leaning on her Beloved. The intimacy that comes with this surrender leads her to declare, "I am my beloved's and my beloved is mine" (Song of Solomon 6:3 NASB).

> This is the real reason for revival: whole-hearted return to the deepest intimacy with your Lover, God, who has waited so long to show all He has in His heart to that one special Bride who will give Him her all. Revival is a return to loving God, I am my Beloved's and He is mine. Nothing else is worth the cost.[6]

I am His and He is mine is covenant language. Our God is a God of covenant, and being joined to Him brings this strong language into the relationship. The Bible tells how the Lord looked upon Israel in the vulnerable time of love and entered a covenant with her. This is a picture of what He desires for you and me.

"Then I passed by you and saw you, and behold, you were [matured] at the time for love; so I spread My skirt over you and covered your nakedness. I also swore to you and entered into a covenant with you so that you became Mine," declares the Lord GOD.

Ezekiel 16:8 NASB

Covenant is an unbreakable agreement between two parties joined to support, provide, protect, and defend. Despite the unfortunate dysfunction and attack on marriage that we see today, marriage is the strongest covenant in our world. In the Bible, when God made a covenant with His people, it was His word and His promise, and He bound Himself to what He said. The devil is after covenant because he is the original covenant breaker! So he releases a spirit of individualism (my way, my will, my terms) aligned with his character and identity to keep people from entering covenant, marriage, and intimacy with Christ. Covenant is a seal, and the enemy knows this. Seals are used to make something official and represent an authority of authenticity and ownership. It is spoken about in Song of Solomon.

Set me like a seal upon your heart, like a seal upon your arm; for love is as strong as death, jealousy is as hard and cruel as Sheol (the place of the dead). Its flashes are flashes of fire, a most vehement flame [the very flame of the Lord]! Many waters cannot quench love, neither can floods drown it.

Song of Solomon 8:6–7 AMPC

Therefore, my brethren, you also have become dead to the law through the body of Christ, that you may be married

90

to another—to Him who was raised from the dead, that we should bear fruit to God.

Romans 7:4

For your Maker is your husband, the LORD of hosts is His name; and your Redeemer is the Holy One of Israel; He is called the God of the whole earth.

Isaiah 54:5

As we have reached the end of this chapter, you may want to stop reading for a moment and renew your vows to the Lord. Renew your covenant and your spiritual pursuit. Evaluate if you've been climbing the wrong hill. Take a moment to renounce loyalties to any other hill. It is a privilege to climb that Holy hill. May we be found leaning on our Beloved.

SIX

Deliverance unto Overcoming

The previous two chapters have dealt with our flesh and carnal desires. The success of our spiritual pursuit requires that we live in complete freedom from fleshly and demonic strongholds. Because of this, we should seek deliverance from these strongholds. But we cannot stop at deliverance—we must move into overcoming. I will touch briefly on both deliverance and overcoming. In Isaiah 61 we see what I call the job description of Jesus when He came to earth.

> The Spirit of the Lord God is upon me, because the Lord has anointed and qualified me to preach the Gospel of good tidings to the meek, the poor, and afflicted; He has sent me to bind up and heal the brokenhearted, to proclaim liberty to the [physical and spiritual] captives and the opening of the prison and of the eyes to those who are bound, to proclaim the acceptable year of the Lord [the year of His favor] and the day of vengeance of our God, to comfort all who mourn, to grant [consolation and joy] to those who mourn

in Zion—to give them an ornament (a garland or diadem) of beauty instead of ashes, the oil of joy instead of mourning, the garment [expressive] of praise instead of a heavy, burdened, and failing spirit—that they may be called oaks of righteousness [lofty, strong, and magnificent, distinguished for uprightness, justice, and right standing with God], the planting of the Lord, that He may be glorified. And they shall rebuild the ancient ruins; they shall raise up the former desolations and renew the ruined cities, the devastations of many generations.

Isaiah 61:1–4 AMPC

And here it is in *The Passion Translation*.

The mighty Spirit of Lord YAHWEH is wrapped around me because YAHWEH has anointed me, as a messenger to preach good news to the poor. He sent me to heal the wounds of the brokenhearted, to tell captives, "You are free," and to tell prisoners, "Be free from your darkness." I am sent to announce a new season of YAHWEH's grace and a time of God's recompense on his enemies, to comfort all who are in sorrow, to strengthen those crushed by despair who mourn in Zion— to give them a beautiful bouquet in the place of ashes, the oil of bliss instead of tears, and the mantle of joyous praise instead of the spirit of heaviness. Because of this, they will be known as Mighty Oaks of Righteousness, planted by YAHWEH as a living display of his glory. They will restore ruins from long ago and rebuild what was long devastated. They will renew ruined cities and desolations of past generations.

Life and choices can leave us with wounds and worries, afflictions and addictions, hurt and heaviness, disappointments

94

and disorders. This is the result of living in a fallen world. These may have been the result of our own decisions or the choices of someone else, but we, or someone we know, has landed in this condition that is real. It is, however, not hopeless.

In our text, we see that a promise is connected to the job description of Jesus. The Holy Spirit has anointed Jesus to set us free and deliver us from all that is listed above—and more. If we read through the end of verse four, we see that our deliverance has an assignment connected to it.

> Because of this, they will be known as Mighty Oaks of Righteousness, planted by YAHWEH as a living display of his glory. They will restore ruins from long ago and rebuild what was long devastated. They will renew ruined cities and desolations of past generations.

If the enemy can keep you locked up in the prison of pain and separated from abundant life, he will keep you from fulfilling God's glory and restoring others who are in the same or similar condition as you. Never forget that your freedom has an assignment connected to it. Others are waiting for you to break free.

You can move to a level of personal deliverance and freedom. You are only as effective as the level of your freedom. Any bondage will be a limitation to fullness in Christ and the fullness of His plan for your life. Before you rationalize that you don't need freedom, think of the last struggle that you had, be it large or small, that you pushed under the proverbial rug, dismissing it as just the usual way

Your freedom has an assignment connected to it.

95

you always feel, react, or behave. Behind every wrong behavior is a corresponding reason. It could be a deep hurt or your uncrucified flesh, but either way, we must desire to be free.

I love the way the Classic Amplified Bible expounds on the quality of life for which Jesus paid the price. "The thief comes only in order to steal and kill and destroy. I came that they may have and enjoy life, and have it in abundance (to the full, till it overflows)" (John 10:10 AMPC).

Quality of life. If the devil can't steal your physical life, he'll attempt to steal, kill, or destroy your quality of life. Because he's an ancient foe who is well acquainted with humankind, he will patiently develop schemes and strategies to overtake and control you. This will make your life less than Christ intended. His primary tool is fear, and his primary battleground is the mind.

If these are conquered by the enemy through any form of bondage, he has control to compromise your quality of life. All he needs is one part of your life to gain control. He does whatever he can do to keep you broken. The good news of Isaiah 61, however, is that with every strategy and scheme of the devil to oppress you and steal your quality of life, there is provision out of bondages and strongholds through Christ, the Anointed One.

The brokenhearted, which means to be crushed completely, are healed.
The captives are set free.
Prison doors are opened.
Those who are bound are liberated.
Those who mourn receive comfort and joy.

Those with ashes receive beauty.

Those who are depressed and heavy receive the relief
of a spirit of expressive praise through the Anointed
One, Christ Jesus.

There is hope today, and it is found in the job description
of Jesus. This is why He came. He came to destroy the works
of the devil and give back your quality of life. His life.

Deliverance is simply the complete elimination of the influence and power of Satan's kingdom over your life. It is
being set free by the power and authority of Jesus Christ from
any form of bondage, stronghold, oppression, possession,
or spiritual captivity. Deliverance is a "from-to" process. It is
when you go from your past iniquity and bondage into freedom. That is when you become delivered. Jesus removes the
total influence that darkness has over
your life, for one purpose: to cause
you to live an abundant life, the highest quality of life to fulfill His destiny
for your life.

There is provision out of bondages and strongholds through Christ.

Jesus' ministry was a ministry of healing and deliverance.
Over and over as He ministered on earth, He set the captive
free from different forms of bondage, even religious bondage. Jesus set them free, and He's still doing so today! We
have this promise. "Now the Lord is the Spirit, and where
the Spirit of the Lord is, there is liberty (emancipation from
bondage, freedom)" (2 Corinthians 3:17 AMPC).

We must be careful, however, not to allow deliverance to
become an end to itself. We are not to seek only deliverance;
we must also pursue overcoming. Deliverance is a moment,
while overcoming is a lifestyle. Deliverance often comes from

desperation. Overcoming is the result of discipline. Deliverance is a necessary moment when strongholds are broken. A stronghold is anything in your life that has a grasp of your mind, will, emotions, or physical body.

A lifestyle of overcoming is one that is cultivated. Both are essential for a successful spiritual pursuit. We will come back to the discipline of overcoming, but we must first understand that the weapons with which we fight to destroy these strongholds are from God. "For the weapons of our warfare are not physical [weapons of flesh and blood], but they are mighty before God for the overthrow and destruction of strongholds" (2 Corinthians 10:4 AMPC).

Deliverance is a moment, while overcoming is a lifestyle.

We have spiritual weapons that have been given to us to move out of bondage into a life of overcoming. The following words written by Max Lucado explain this concept.

> Does one prevailing problem stalk your life? Where does Satan have a hook in you? Some are prone to cheat. Others quick to doubt. Maybe you worry. . . . Perhaps you are judgmental. . . . Where does the devil have a stronghold on you? Ahh, there is the word that fits—stronghold—fortress, citadel, thick walls, tall gates. It's as if the devil has fenced in one negative attribute, one bad habit, one weakness and constructed a rampart around it. . . . We do not grit our teeth and redouble our efforts. No, this is the way of the flesh. Our weapons are from God. They have divine power to demolish strongholds.[1]

If you're going to experience full deliverance, you must believe in God's weapons above your own ideas and culture's ideas. It takes divine power to demolish every stronghold. It's time to trust in the power of God. Where you put your time is where you put your trust. Is it in the Word? In prayer? In the revelation that God is able? Or is it in some other natural source, such as a person or an idea? While we have many amazing intelligent people on this planet, there is only one power that can destroy fortresses erected by the devil—God's power!

Strongholds come through traps of the enemy, generational iniquities, and willful sin. Once a stronghold is established, it takes the power of God to dislodge and deliver us. These strongholds manifest in our mind, will, emotions, and physical bodies. They present struggles, behavioral issues, wrong belief patterns, sicknesses that are inordinate, relationship issues, and more. In short, they steal our quality of life. But we have a promise of freedom in the Word of God. "[Rather] is not this the fast that I have chosen: to loose the bonds of wickedness, to undo the bands of the yoke, to let the oppressed go free, and that you break every [enslaving] yoke?" (Isaiah 58:6 AMPC). The Good News that Jesus preached is restoration of life, the quality of life that comes from His life. This is not just an adjustment or a temporary fix, but it involves breaking every enslaving yoke!

> It's time to trust in the power of God.

Let's go a step further today, from deliverance into an overcoming life. Overcoming is a lifestyle and a choice. A number of years ago, I was attending a conference, and I heard and have never forgotten the phrase that every choice is a seed, and every seed will bear fruit. Each choice we make brings a harvest. You are living today in the harvest of yesterday's choices. This is a sobering thought. In our context, once you've tasted deliverance, you must choose overcoming. Both deliverance and overcoming take faith, but at different levels.

Deliverance often comes out of desperation, which is a necessary and beautiful thing. We find ourselves in a desperate situation or time in our lives where possibly we have hit rock bottom. At this desperate place, we cry out for deliverance. God will always come and set us free. To stay in that place of freedom and to grow in an overcoming life, however, we must continue to cry out with the same desperation that helped us receive deliverance.

The devil will taunt and tempt, you can count on it. He doesn't leave you alone simply because you have been delivered. You will need to develop a strong resolve to stay free and to move into greater levels of spiritual growth. Here are a few verses that can move us to overcome.

> Leave no [such] room or foothold for the devil [give no opportunity to him].
>
> Ephesians 4:27 AMPC

> In [this] freedom Christ has made us free [and completely liberated us]; stand fast then, and do not be hampered and held ensnared and submit again to a yoke of slavery [which you have once put off].
>
> Galatians 5:1 AMPC

> Do not love or cherish the world or the things that are in the world. If anyone loves the world, love for the Father is not in him. For all that is in the world—the lust of the flesh [craving for sensual gratification] and the lust of the eyes [greedy longings of the mind] and the pride of life [assurance in one's

own resources or in the stability of earthly things]—these do not come from the Father but are from the world [itself]. And the world passes away and disappears, and with it the forbidden cravings (the passionate desires, the lust) of it; but he who does the will of God and carries out His purposes in his life abides (remains) forever.

1 John 2:15–17 AMPC

And they have overcome (conquered) him by means of the blood of the Lamb and by the utterance of their testimony, for they did not love and cling to life even when faced with death [holding their lives cheap till they had to die for their witnessing].

Revelation 12:11 AMPC

"Catch the foxes for us, the little foxes that are ruining the vineyards, while our vineyards are in blossom."

Song of Solomon 2:15 NASB

He who overcomes, I will grant to him to sit down with Me on My throne, as I also overcame and sat down with My Father on His throne.

Revelation 3:21 NASB

You are not supposed to be a rollercoaster Christian, up one day and down the next. You are also not to be an in-and-out Christian (in church one week and out the next). This is not an abundant life. This is not making the choices of an overcomer. You have been given everything you need for life and godliness (see 2 Peter 1:3). As you make the right choices that lead to righteousness and wholeness according to the

Word of God, you will find that you walk in a level place in your life. "Teach me Your way, LORD, and lead me on a level path because of my enemies" (Psalm 27:11 NASB2020).

Pray these verses and others like them daily to keep you steady, stable, and overcoming!

SEVEN

The Cycle of Revival

Do not be deceived, God is not mocked; for whatever a man sows, that he will also reap. For he who sows to his flesh will of the flesh reap corruption, but he who sows to the Spirit will of the Spirit reap everlasting life. And let us not grow weary while doing good, for in due season we shall reap if we do not lose heart.

Galatians 6:7–9

You cannot grow weary in your pursuit, as there are many due seasons in your personal, sustained revival. It is your continual sowing that creates a continual harvest of spiritual growth. Your due season is about reaping what you have sown. You have an appointed harvest, which is why you cannot break the cycle. A cycle is a series of disciplines and consecrations that are regularly repeated in the same order. A harvest is waiting for your seed, and your seed is waiting for you to sow it. You can't grow weary, and you cannot break the cycle.

Revival is living in a continual zealous pursuit of God and His presence that affects and transforms all areas of your life and lifestyle. It is eternal in the sense that it does not end, because the pursuit never ends. Even in eternity, we will forever pursue Jesus through our worship.

Unfortunately, in our modern Church mindset, we've been conditioned to a formula or method that does not fit with an eternal revival concept. We've got time limits and structural limits that are both spoken and unspoken. Typically, in the Church, we do not think long term when it comes to revival.

Can a lifelong pursuit of revival be possible? Only if you will commit to the cycle of revival, a series of disciplines and consecrations that are regularly repeated in the same order, which is a lifelong pursuit of Him. This pursuit is ever-changing and usually looks like nothing of this temporal world.

This is where we falter. We're looking for an end or a destination in revival, where it's a journey without end. It's a continual cycle of repeated disciplines, consecration, and sacrifices that will take us higher and deeper with Christ. We incorrectly assume that when it gets too hard for our flesh, revival must be over. Or, if things seem to wane and we're not as excited about it as we used to be, then revival must be over.

So the only option left to us is to go back to normal. Go back to comfort and ease. Could it be possible that revivals of the past were determined to be over because no one did the hard work of breaking up the new level of fallow ground to break through to a new level of revival? Sustaining revival in your life doesn't get easier, it gets harder. It was the life of the prophets, Jesus, and the apostles. Why should we think it would be anything less for us?

So if we refuse the cycle of revival, we then begin to adopt new ways of looking like we're experiencing revival, which is religion. Without the pain and process of breaking up the new ground of our heart both personal and corporate, we look like we're in revival when we're far from it. We're tired of shedding tears and laying our lives as a sacrifice. When this happens, we experience emptiness that pervades personal and corporate atmospheres and reflects a break in the cycle.

Revival has no breaks. If you break from revival, you're no longer in revival. It is a true takeover of all parts of our lives and churches. Revival is all or nothing. This phrase means doing something completely and fully or nothing at all. True revival demands our all!

So let's dive into the cycle in the hope that this will keep you in a fresh pursuit of personal revival.

The Pain of Revival—The Breakdown of the Flesh

The acts of the flesh are obvious: sexual immorality, impurity and debauchery; idolatry and witchcraft; hatred, discord, jealousy, fits of rage, selfish ambition, dissensions, factions and envy; drunkenness, orgies, and the like. I warn you, as I did before, that those who live like this will not inherit the kingdom of God.

Galatians 5:19–21 NIV

Those who belong to Christ Jesus have crucified the flesh with its passions and desires.

Galatians 5:24 NIV

For revival to sustain in your personal pursuit of God, you must be ready for a continual crucifixion of your flesh. Your flesh must die daily, as Paul said (see 1 Corinthians 15:13). Your flesh is your soulish realm, your mind, will, and emotions. This part of you must continually give up full control for revival to do its fullest work. Take a look at how this looked in the life of the prophet Isaiah. This may be a view you've not seen before.

> In the year that King Uzziah died, I saw the Lord sitting on a throne, high and lifted up, and the train of His robe filled the temple. . . . So I said:
>
>> "Woe is me, for I am undone!
>> Because I am a man of unclean lips,
>> And I dwell in the midst of a people of unclean lips;
>> For my eyes have seen the King, the LORD of hosts."
>
> Then one of the seraphim flew to me, having in his hand a live coal which he had taken with the tongs from the altar. And he touched my mouth with it, and said:
>
>> "Behold, this has touched your lips;
>> your iniquity is taken away,
>> And your sin purged."
>
> Also I heard the voice of the Lord, saying:
>
>> "Whom shall I send,
>> And who will go for Us?"
>
> Then I said, "Here am I! Send me."
> And He said, "Go, and tell this people:
>
>> 'Keep on hearing, but do not understand;
>> Keep on seeing, but do not perceive.'

> Make the heart of this people dull,
> And their ears heavy,
> And shut their eyes;
> Lest they see with their eyes,
> And hear with their ears,
> And understand with their heart,
> And return and be healed."

Then I said, "Lord, how long?"
And He answered:

> "Until the cities are laid waste and without
> inhabitant,
> The houses are without a man,
> The land is utterly desolate,
> The LORD has removed men far away,
> And the forsaken places are many in the midst of the
> land."
>
> Isaiah 6:1–12

This passage is quoted five times in the New Testament. When Isaiah asked how long he was to keep declaring this prophetic word, the Lord said *until*. We must develop an *until* mindset. Until is an undefined amount of time. It is as long as an object or goal needs pursuing. As long as it takes and whatever it takes. Until is up to the time that you accomplish the goal of the Lord for that time or season. It means that you continue until. This mindset is absolutely imperative in the cycle of revival.

The revelation that Isaiah had when he saw the Lord led him to an unconditional response of crying out *hineni*. In Hebrew, this word means, "Here am I."[1] Here am I, Lord,

send me! The unconditional *here am I* came as a result of
seeing the Lord. When Isaiah was called to an until assignment, he didn't waver because he had seen
We must develop   the Lord. The fire had touched his flesh, and
an until mindset.   he was never the same.

      If you take the first part out of our passage
in Isaiah and only grab hold of the latter, you'll lose the full
impact of the call of Isaiah to "until." When we labor out
of knowledge rather than revelation, we will never complete
an until assignment. All that we do will be out of duty and
obligation. Remember, this is a lifelong pursuit of the Lord.
Your ability to adopt an until revelation will be the key to
your success.

      The labor of the "here am I" must be done from the pos-
ture of undone. Undone in this context speaks of complete
and utter ruin. It's your flesh being pulled into pieces until
destruction. This sounds painful and devastating, but it is
a victory.

      Ironically, the angel touched the most gifted part of Isaiah,
his mouth. Remember that he was a prophet. Yet even after
many prophecies, he realized after seeing the Lord that his
most gifted part was unclean. I hope you realize that Isaiah
had to have a renewal in the cycle. So do we.

      Your flesh can keep you from your until. The revival cycle
includes this crucial element of a touch of the fire from the
altar of God around the throne of God to the most delicate
and prized areas of our lives. If this doesn't happen, we will
continue in a revival pursuit with the posture of pride, which
only produces religion—form without power, appearance
without substance, fanfare without fire. We must live in the
state of undone.

There are too many believers who skip the "I saw the Lord" phase and are joining in on the "Here am I, send me!" People tend to serve out of a duty rather than a revelation. When we reach the part where God told Isaiah to do this until, our deficit is revealed.

It is much easier to *do* than to *become undone*. We cannot do things for revival and be a revivalist or be in personal revival. There is only one thing that constitutes as being a revivalist and in revival: the permeating presence of God being in absolute control of every area of our lives. We live in a state of perpetually undone. Ruined flesh!

Don't skip the stage of "undone," the breakdown of the flesh. It is the pain of revival and a part that is necessary on our spiritual pursuit. Revival starts with undone or repentance: Woe is me, not woe is everyone else. If we can't see our own unclean part, we're not in

> It is much easier to do than to become undone.

a place of revival. Never forget that God doesn't wink at our sin, overlook it, or dismiss it as part of our humanity. Jesus paid the price for us to walk free of a life of sin with His blood. Thankfully, He has given us the opportunity to repent.

Repentance is a blessing. The Lord told David that He desires truth in the inner being (see Psalm 51:6). Paul said that he dies daily (see 1 Corinthians 15:31). Many look at repentance as negative when in reality it is the most powerful, merciful gift the Lord has given us. It is the opportunity to confess our sins and shortcomings so that we can stay on the walk of revival.

Sin separates us from God, which we see in the Garden of Eden. *Where are you, Adam?* was asked as a direct result of sin that had stopped the walk of revival. *We were walking well together, Adam. What happened?* One cannot expect to sustain personal revival with willful sin allowed in his or her life. We must take a strong look at sin and an equally strong look at repentance so that we can stay desperate. God doesn't wink at sin. Our current loose culture within the Church, not to mention outside the Church, is accepting of a lot of things that God doesn't accept. We must call a sin a sin and repent so that we continue to walk in the zeal of revival fire every day.

The first part of the cycle is crucial, which is the inclination to skip the *woe* just to get to the *go*. This is trying to have revival without pain. There is no such thing!

The pain and pressure of the stage of undone is what keeps us in the next stages of the cycle of revival. Undone is an unraveling of flesh that allows us to make it through the *until* season. "How long do I do this, Lord?" Isaiah asked. The Lord answered, *Until*. If we are walking with self-preservation, we will never make it forward. We will be our own hindrance in revival.

What is your posture in the until? If it's anything other than undone, you'll never make it in revival. If you don't see Him, you'll not be able to bear the weight of revival. You'll try to advance, but because of your deficit (not your gift or your amount of serving, but your spiritual deficit) you'll not live an until revival life.

If you don't grow with revival, it will outgrow you. Isaiah was a burning man, and only burning men and women will say without hesitation and unconditionally, Here am I. Send me. This stage of the cycle develops an unquestionable and unconditional sacrifice within us that is needed in the next stage of the cycle.

The Plow of Revival—Break up the Fallow Ground

"Ephraim is a trained heifer that loves to thresh grain; but I harnessed her fair neck, I will make Ephraim pull a plow. Judah shall plow; Jacob shall break his clods." Sow for yourselves righteousness; reap in mercy; break up your fallow ground, for it is time to seek the LORD, till He comes and rains righteousness on you.

Hosea 10:11–12

As we sow the seeds of revival, we mustn't sow in bad soil. It needs to be broken up. You may say that your soil is fine, and to that I ask, Where is the fruit?

For thus says the LORD to the men of Judah and Jerusalem: "Break up your fallow ground, and do not sow among thorns. Circumcise yourselves to the LORD, and take away the foreskins of your hearts."

Jeremiah 4:3–4

Revival seldom occurs entirely by Sovereign initiative. Individual human and corporate will must be activated before the fruits of revival and harvest will manifest. The fallow ground represents the hardened heart not yet prepared for the implantation of the seeds of God's word. The wording in this verse implies the personal responsibility one must take.[2]

Fallow ground is uncultivated ground or soil that is allowed to lie useless and unproductive. The inference is that this ground was once fertile but is now fallow or hardened, so much that it is not ready for the next level of revival. So Hosea tells us that we are to seek Him until. There's the word *until* again. The resolute thread that holds personal, sustained revival together is until.

Again, until is an undefined amount of time, as long as you need to keep doing it until you see it. It is as long as it takes and whatever it takes. Until is up to the time that you continue until. Hosea and Jeremiah tell us that to reach the next level of revival, we're going to need to recognize, admit, and confess that there is uncultivated ground in front of us. Unless we pull, plow, and break, we'll not reach the next level of revival. We can't opt out—it must be cultivated. We cannot skip this step. Remember that individual human and corporate will must be activated before the fruits of revival and harvest will manifest. There is an ongoing personal responsibility to *pull, plow,* and *break.*

> Do not be deceived, God is not mocked; for whatever a man sows, that he will also reap. For he who sows to his flesh will of the flesh reap corruption, but he who sows to the Spirit will of the Spirit reap everlasting life. And let us not grow weary while doing good, for in due season [until] we shall reap if we do not lose heart.
>
> Galatians 6:7–9

> Those who sow in tears shall reap in joy. He who continually goes forth weeping, bearing seed for sowing, shall doubtless come again with rejoicing, bringing his sheaves with him.
>
> Psalm 126:5–6

When you stop sowing in revival, you stop reaping in revival. When you stop weeping in revival, you stop bearing seed in revival. The sowing and the weeping (brokenness, humility, undone) keep us in this cycle of revival and allow it to sustain.

In Hosea it says, "I will make Ephraim *pull* a plow. Judah shall *plow*; Jacob shall *break* his clods" (Hosea 10:11, emphasis added). The clods here speak of resistance to staying in the cycle. Some reach a clod and stop. You must learn to break them up and not break the cycle.

Each of these verbs imply work. Sustained revival in your personal life and in the corporate setting is work because sustained revival doesn't get easier. It gets harder, because you're going from glory to glory. With each new level of glory, you are required another trip around the cycle of revival, the pain of the flesh to the plowing of the hard places in our hearts. It is at this stage, the breaking of the uncultivated ground, that we must draw from our revelation of seeing the Lord and be resolved. The temptation to waffle and digress will be the greatest yet. The tests and temptations will come to see how well you know how to pull, plow, and break. In your spiritual pursuit, don't run from the mundane. Stop looking for the spectacular and simply *pull*, *plow*, and *break*.

This is an individual responsibility that includes fresh seeking of personal revival. We have some clods of resistance that need to be broken up and moved out of the way for the seed of the Word to produce fruit. These clods represent things such as fear, slothfulness, familiarity, carnality, or ambition, to name a few. These things act as resistance or stumbling blocks to your passionate pursuit. There is no time to whine. Just plow. In this world, you will have tribulations. Don't be like the children of Israel in the wilderness, whining their way through. It's time to plow.

This will be a stage of the cycle when you're typically tested on how you do in trials and temptations. This stage will test your humility and whether or not you remember seeing the Lord and how undone you were. This is all a part of breaking up your fallow ground. Pass the test. Pull, plow, and break. You will be tempted to trade zeal for intentions. True zeal is unconditional, but intentions come with an attitude of *if I feel like it.*

Stop looking for the spectacular and simply pull, plow, and break.

Your interest versus intentions will be tested in this stage of the cycle. Your interests cause you to be invested, while many judge themselves by their intentions. I believe many are living a happy life because they have the intention to pull, plow, and break, but so many other things take precedence, and the ground is never broken up to lead them to the rain of righteousness. Intentions do not break fallow ground. Pull, plow, and break!

In this stage you'll feel very weary or tired. Count on it. If you do not focus on pulling, plowing, and breaking, you will turn inward. This is where a lot of revivalists lose sight of His presence, and they stop breaking the clods of resistance. When that happens, we become a hindrance to sustained, personal revival. We can never lose sight of the deeper spiritual cultivation in sustained revival. The process doesn't just involve a few altar calls before we've completed our responsibility. Rather, it involves constant plowing of uncultivated ground. And here is a crucial key: "But those who wait on the LORD shall renew their strength; they shall mount up with wings like eagles, they shall run and not be weary, they shall walk and not faint" (Isaiah 40:31).

114

Can a lifelong pursuit of revival be possible? If you learn to pull, plow and break, the answer is yes. If you do not, then you'll burn out by bowing to your own circumstances. Everything within you will be tested. Do you really want to be in personal revival? This is the plow of revival. Break up the fallow ground or you'll not move forward! A continual engagement of God in your life and your lifestyle. The cycle of revival. The great revivalist Charles Finney said, "Revival comes from heaven when heroic souls enter the conflict determined to win or die—or if need be, to win and die!"[3]

The Product of Revival—The Breakthrough to Fruit

If you're faithful to the pain and the plow, you will break through to the fruit of revival. This is the goal of personal revival. What is the fruit of revival? "Those who sow in tears shall reap in joy. He who continually goes forth weeping, bearing seed for sowing, shall doubtless come again with rejoicing, bringing his sheaves with him" (Psalm 126:5–6).

The fruit of revival is joy, more seed to sow, rejoicing, and harvest. Be patient; harvest is coming. Does a tree bear fruit once? No. Every year it has a cycle of new growth. If it didn't work that way, the tree would not produce new fruit. Every season, it should grow fresh fruit.

Here is a humorous story to illustrate this point. My granddaughter, River, who was four years old at the time, joined us at our house. During her stay, she decided to take a sweet potato from our pantry and wrap it in a piece of her clothing. She was pretending to be shopping with a small toy shopping cart. We did not know, however, that she had wrapped up the sweet potato. When the toys were put away, the potato stayed wrapped in that piece of clothing for an unknown amount of time. My husband stumbled upon it one day. It was so decayed that we couldn't even recognize what it was! We couldn't recognize that it was a sweet potato.

With this story in mind, ask yourself if you are carrying old fruit. It could possibly stink. Old fruit is the kind that causes you to look like you have it all together when you really have no life or vitality. Old fruit makes you a cranky revivalist. Old fruit causes dissatisfaction, disengagement, and disagreement. Often those attitudes are because you are tired of this cycle. Old fruit produces stale atmospheres in your pursuit of Him. The health of the spiritual fruit will be seen in your attitude, your faithfulness to the Lord and His Word, the health of your family, your zeal, your choices, and your unity.

Revival cannot have a bubble in which we stay isolated and protected, even excluded from the cycle. In other words, we cannot stay in a particular stage when we're on a lifelong journey in revival. We must break out of where we are and move into fresh fruit!

If you are not seeing fruit, then transformation has stopped in your life, and you've left revival. Just knowing about revival is not enough. Just hanging out with others in revival is not enough. There is a journey of revival that requires real sacrifice of all or nothing. Don't be your own resistance in revival growth and then blame your lack of results on other people. If you're not internally producing fresh fruit, you will be a rotting revivalist. It's time to break through to fruit, the product of revival.

Remember, this is the cycle of revival, a series of disciplines and consecrations that are regularly repeated in the same order. There is the confrontation of your flesh, the cultivation of the soil of your heart, and the consistency of bearing fresh fruit. All of this will determine your due season. You will reap if you do not faint. Keep pulling, keep plowing, and keep breaking.

The cycle of revival.

EIGHT

The Necessity of Tongues

I want you to be empowered to continue your spiritual pursuit, to stay desperate, and to continue to dig deeper in the Spirit. Remember, revival is a long walk; therefore, you need to stay spiritually strengthened and maintain a burning heart and a passion for Jesus and His mission. One very powerful tool to which we have access is the baptism in the Holy Spirit with the evidence of speaking in other tongues.

> When the day of Pentecost had come, they were all together in one place. And suddenly there came from heaven a noise like a violent rushing wind, and it filled the whole house where they were sitting. And there appeared to them tongues as of fire distributing themselves, and they rested on each one of them. And they were all filled with the Holy Spirit and began to speak with other tongues, as the Spirit was giving them utterance.
>
> Acts 2:1–4 NASB

On the Day of Pentecost, an amazing transaction happened where God came in the form of supernatural fire that

119

landed on 120 people, and they were baptized in the Holy Spirit with the evidence of speaking in other tongues as the Spirit gave them utterance. I fully believe that Jesus knew that what would be required of them *after* the Upper Room would be fueled by what they received *in* the Upper Room. On your spiritual pursuit, don't try to go out before you go up! The Upper Room is where power, fire, and a heavenly sound that you will need later is waiting for you.

To clarify, there is the indwelling Holy Spirit when we receive Christ as Savior, then there is a subsequent baptism, or immersion of the Holy Spirit, that requires another level of yielding. The initial evidence of that baptism is speaking in tongues as the Spirit gives utterance. We see this clearly in the Word of

Don't try to go out before you go up!

God. Jesus breathed on His disciples before His crucifixion and resurrection, and then the Holy Spirit was poured out on them in the Upper Room. The result was an immersion in God's presence and an introduction to the wonderful third Person of the Godhead, who is called *paraclete*, meaning One who goes along beside or to call beside in the sense of a lawyer. He is an Advocate, Counselor, and Comforter.

> But the Comforter (Counselor, Helper, Intercessor, Advocate, Strengthener, Standby), the Holy Spirit, Whom the Father will send in My name [in My place, to represent Me and act on My behalf], He will teach you all things. And He will cause you to recall (will remind you of, bring to your remembrance) everything I have told you.
>
> John 14:26 AMPC

When Jesus launched His Church, a mantle fell from heaven. He clothed, defined, and distinguished His Church with a mantle. He didn't leave us uncovered. He's been covering us since the Fall of man in the Garden with leaves, tents, and veils—until the Cross. At that moment, the veil was torn, and we received free access to the Father. All that was in His realm was granted. On the Day of Pentecost, He designed the covering to be as it was in the Garden, which was a covering of unhindered power, glory, and fire. His presence came in fullness on the Day of Pentecost as He always intended it to be. With that visitation, Jesus defines and distinguishes His Church.

He didn't leave us exposed to be defined by any other mantle, or to fall short of His glory. He caused a heavenly wind to stir a heavenly mantle to drop from His realm into our realm, and it manifested and set upon them in the form of fire! Don't miss that the fire, unlike the wind, sat upon them. It was their mantle. The fire from around His Throne and in His eyes was now in their hearts. And the evidence was that they spoke with tongues! These firebrands were carriers of a mantle that their Upper Room pursuit had produced. It produced a revival fire, which had an impact on everything they touched.

God wants to use you to do the same. Do you have a viable, consistent Upper Room pursuit? This is still where the mantle of fire falls. Jesus told them this mantle of fire would go into all the world, which shows us that Jesus never intended for this fire to go out. A vital part of our spiritual pursuit is about keeping that fire of Pentecost ablaze in our hearts.

God was very specific in His Word that His fire was to be a perpetual fire. A sustained fire. There has been a holy flame ablaze and lit by God Himself that has forever burned.

This flame represents the essence of God, who He is, what He carries within, and what He displays without.

There came a time in the scope of eternity where God said that it was time to share this flame, and God broke into the earth as fire. First, we see it in the Old Testament:

> Then fire came out from before the LORD and consumed the burnt offering and the portions of fat on the altar; and when all the people saw it, they shouted and fell on their faces.
>
> Leviticus 9:24 NASB

> But the fire on the altar must be kept burning on it; it must not be quenched. And the priest must burn wood every morning on it, and he shall arrange the burnt offering on it, and he shall turn into smoke the fat portions of the fellowship offerings on it. A perpetual fire must be kept burning on the altar; it must not be quenched.
>
> Leviticus 6:12–13 LEB

God was and still is very serious about this flame. In Leviticus, His directive was to keep the fire burning on the altar. He wanted a perpetual fire. All throughout the Word of God, we see Him sending a reminder of this original flame endorsed by His name. The fire on the altar in Leviticus became the fire on Mount Horeb, then the pillar of fire by night seen on Mount Carmel, then within Jeremiah's bones, in the wheels of Ezekiel, and within the fire of the refiner in Malachi. The fire that fell on the disciples on the Day of Pentecost became the moment in time that God chose to give His Church a mantle. The symbolism was this same fire from

Leviticus. I repeat this to emphasize a primary point for your spiritual pursuit: He wants a sustained fire.

The perpetual fire of the Old Testament became the Pentecostal fire in the New Testament. The directive still stands—you are never to let the flame on the altar go out. The altar is your heart, and it is your responsibility. Is it burning today? Have you kept the fire burning on the altar of your heart? When the Holy Ghost makes His entrance, He brings a rush of power and passion. The initial reception is exciting and refreshing; however, it's one thing to be a fire-starter and an entirely different thing to be a fire-keeper!

The original flame on the altar in Leviticus burned for 860 years until someone let it go out. I don't want the fire to go out on my watch. How about you? Generations yet to be born are counting on us to keep the flame alive. When people look at your spiritual walk, do they see you burn? Do they see your burning heart, and do they hear the sounds of Pentecost in your voice? Do they hear the passion, the zeal, and the burden of the Lord that the early Church carried?

He wants a sustained fire.

This fire that came on the early Church would come to represent zeal, fervor, and passion that would compel and propel them to the ends of the earth as they knew it. They became firebrands, which is one who ignites, stirs, kindles, agitates, and instigates. A firebrand is an enemy of status quo spirituality who spends his or her days provoking others to burn for Him.

Whatever the Holy Spirit was first, He is now and will remain forever the same. What He did then, He wants to do now, for His power has not diminished. He came with wind and fire, which resulted in utterances and prophetic anointings. He still wants to burn in and blow on His Church. May we be found inviting Him on our spiritual pursuit to come like a flame of fire, a mighty rushing wind!

Way too many have made Him a flicker instead of a flame. They have made Him a breeze instead of a wind. In doing so, they have grieved Him by making Him much less in the earth today than when He came on the Day of Pentecost. The Holy Spirit was not temporary, and the display of His power was not to be seen once and no more. He is still in the earth, and we have the privilege of being able to expect Him to manifest and work as He did on that day. If He does not currently manifest in the presence and power of Pentecost in our lives, we should search ourselves to see what is in our lives that might be hindering Him. Is there something within us that is stifling or vexing Him so that His power and fire cannot be released today as it was on that day?

I want to be both challenging and inspirational, because I know that something must be lit in you before you'll truly pursue the mantle for sustained fire in your spiritual pursuit. The fact that Jesus told the early Church that this mantle of fire would go into all the world shows us that Jesus never intended this fire to go out. Just like us, however, they had to choose to keep the fire burning. One of the key ways we accomplish this is by utilizing the gift that was given on the Day of Pentecost—praying in tongues.

Before you speak *for* Him, you first must speak *to* Him. There are many advantages to speaking in tongues, and one of the greatest is that it is a language given to us from God that speaks directly to Him. Now tell me, what better tool can you have as you're pursuing God than to have a language that speaks directly to Him? This element is vital to the desperate seeker as this is your connection to the deeper realms of God by the Spirit of God. "For he who speaks in a tongue does not speak to men but to God, for no one understands him; however, in the spirit he speaks mysteries" (1 Corinthians 14:2).

From this posture and in this language, we have the ability and privilege to access the Throne Room and all the revelation and wisdom it contains. We have access to God's heart and mind. We have an unending supply of His spiritual riches and treasures. Prayer in tongues releases power for Christian living, for our spiritual pursuit, and for all that we are called to do for the Kingdom of God. "But you shall receive power (ability, efficiency, and might) when the Holy Spirit has come upon you, and you shall be My witnesses in Jerusalem and all Judea and Samaria and to the ends (the very bounds) of the earth" (Acts 1:8 AMPC).

It is important to note that the Amplified version says that this power from the Holy Spirit brings ability, efficiency, and might. Remember that people were astonished at Jesus' teaching because it was delivered with ability, authority, weight, and power. Jesus was filled with the same Holy Spirit. How do we access this? Through the power of the Holy Spirit. This is the necessity of tongues.

When you speak to God in tongues, He speaks back to you in the Spirit. It is from this wealth and reservoir of spiritual tongues that we walk in authority, boldness, wisdom, and power that cannot be accessed anywhere else. We are literally houses of the language of heaven!

I have seen the decline of speaking in tongues within the Spirit-filled church because their people have become ashamed of it. They are ashamed because of our perceived thought that it will offend. The arguments for and against it are broad. What I want you to take away from this is that the phenomenon of speaking in tongues is integral to the disciples being filled with the Spirit. If you take tongues out of Acts 2, the outcome of the Day of Pentecost is deeply altered. Tongues were an intentional part of the sounds of Pentecost.

You are filled with the Spirit when you speak in tongues. There are other evidences of the filling of the Holy Spirit that should be cultivated, but the initial evidence is speaking in tongues. We see this clearly in Acts 2. On that day, the disciples spoke in supernaturally inspired utterances that were recognizable languages; however, there is no indication later in the Acts and New Testament that the languages were understood or identified. The Greek word for tongues is *glossa*, which means "language." And the apostle Paul said that our tongue given by the Spirit *speaks to God*. It is a language that He gives us to communicate with Him to speak mysteries that need to be released. Without this heavenly language, we would have no means to release the inexpressible sounds of heaven. What are these mysteries to which I refer? Corey Russell, in his book *The Glory Within*, explains:

> The word *mystery* refers to those things that were hidden in the heart of God throughout the Old Testament and unveiled through the ministry of Christ and the revelation of the Holy Spirit. . . . We were made to discover the deep things of God. . . . As we speak in tongues . . . we are speaking heavenly things that our minds do not yet understand, but as we pray in the Spirit, God releases these mysteries through our mouths and into our spirits so we may receive the deep things of His heart.[1]

Proverbs tells us, "It is the glory of God to conceal a matter, but the glory of kings is to search out a matter" (25:2 NASB). Russell goes on to say that the search isn't about God keeping things hidden *from* us. We know that He is keeping them hidden *for* us. It is in the search for those mysteries that we cultivate a deeper, abiding relationship with Him. When we seek His mysteries, we encounter Him.

> He designed our hearts to run on fresh encounter and fresh revelation. . . . The majority of the mysteries that we release through speaking in tongues fit into these four categories. . . . I am speaking mysteries about God. . . . I am speaking mysteries about myself. . . . I am speaking mysteries about His plans. . . . I am speaking mysteries about people in need.[2]

The success of your spiritual pursuit will require that you search things out in the Spirit. This is part of uncovering the mysteries of God. Don't allow this type of verbiage to overwhelm you or to puff you up. The simple reality is that God wants us to discover more of Him, and that discovery is fueled by a passionate desire to know Him at deeper levels. Much of this cannot be articulated with natural words. It is something that can only be experienced and tasted in the Spirit. This is what we are instructed to do. "O taste and see that the LORD is good; how blessed is the man who takes refuge in Him!" (Psalm 34:8 NASB).

When we seek His mysteries, we encounter Him.

Your spiritual language of tongues unlocks the deeper levels of God. In the context of prayer, when we reach the end of our natural utterance, this supernatural utterance takes over and accomplishes much more than we can ever imagine.

> In the same way the Spirit also helps our weakness; for we do not know how to pray as we should, but the Spirit Himself intercedes for us with groanings too deep for words; and He who searches the hearts knows what the mind of the Spirit is, because He intercedes for the saints according to the will of God.
>
> Romans 8:26–27 NASB

He helps in our areas of weakness or when our level of understanding comes up short. The Amplified Bible describes the way He speaks for us with the words *unspeakable yearnings* and *groanings too deep for utterance*. He searches our hearts, then He inspires us to release a tongue or a wordless utterance that speaks exactly what needs to be unlocked, prayed, or released. This is a powerful tool on our spiritual journey.

Another asset to speaking and praying in tongues is that it builds you up in your spirit man. There is a spiritual capacity increase that transpires when you pray in the spirit. "But you, beloved, build yourselves up [founded] on your most holy faith [make progress, rise like an edifice higher and higher], praying in the Holy Spirit" (Jude 20 AMPC). This version states that you make progress.

What are we talking about in this book? The power of pursuit. A pursuit is a journey, and the Bible says that praying in the Holy Spirit helps you make progress. What an undeniable necessary tool for progress on your pursuit!

This verse also says that we rise higher and higher. In the previous chapters, we explored that our ultimate goal is to ascend higher into His realm to access more. Jude tells us that the way we accomplish that goal is by praying in the Holy Spirit. If we're going to stay desperate for God, we need this vital gift that opens the realms of His presence—the language of heaven—to stay on fire for Him.

> Now on the final and most important day of the Feast, Jesus stood, and He cried in a loud voice, If any man is thirsty, let him come to Me and drink! He who believes in Me [who cleaves to and trusts in and relies on Me] as the Scripture has said, From his innermost being shall flow [continuously] springs and rivers of living water. But He was speaking here of the Spirit, Whom those who believed (trusted, had faith) in Him were afterward to receive. For the [Holy] Spirit had not yet been given, because Jesus was not yet glorified (raised to honor).
>
> John 7:37–39 AMPC

What a powerful passage with so much in it for our spiritual pursuit. First, we see that praying in tongues quenches a spiritual thirst. It is like a continuous flow of fresh living water that comes from our spirit, our innermost being. Second, when we pray in tongues, we receive a release of life from His realm. We are built up, and we carry the life of God.

Heaven has a lot of living water. It flows from the throne, and it never stops. The Bible calls it a river. In the natural, when we look at a river, we don't see the same water twice. It is flowing, and its movements are ever-changing. It is the same in the spiritual realm. There are new revelations, new encounters, new stamina, new resolve, and an ever-flowing new life that flows in this heavenly river. This is the necessity of tongues in our spiritual pursuit.

Maybe you're reading this right now and have never been baptized in the Holy Ghost. If you've received Jesus as Savior and Lord of your life, you only need to ask for this gift. It is a gift given freely to those who are hungry and who will yield to the Spirit. Pray this prayer out loud:

Jesus, You are the baptizer in the Holy Ghost. I believe this gift is for me as promised in Your Word. I ask to be filled with Your Spirit with the evidence of speaking in other tongues. I yield to You now, and by faith I receive. In Jesus' name, Amen.

As you worship the Lord, be sensitive to His presence. He will come and take control, if you allow Him. He will use your natural tongue and voice to express supernatural tongues. Give Him full control.

NINE

The Burning Place

Something radical and impactful happens when you meet Jesus *on the road*. What could I possibly mean by that? In the gospel of Luke, we see two men on their way to a town called Emmaus. The name *Emmaus* means "the burning place." These men walked beside Jesus, yet their eyes could not see Him. True revival is seeing Jesus. It is possible to have a pursuit yet follow so far behind that you cannot *see* Him. If we're not intentional, our pursuit can turn into a form, façade, or familiarity with Jesus that causes us to be blinded by religion and miss the crucial entry to revival, which is seeing Jesus. How does this happen? When our pursuit is merely about checking the boxes instead of checking our heart and closeness with Jesus, our pursuit will fade into a form. This is religion, and it brings spiritual blindness.

Here's the story of these two men making their way to the burning place.

Now behold, two of them were traveling that same day to a village called Emmaus, which was seven miles from Jerusalem. And they talked together of all these things which had happened. So it was, while they conversed and reasoned, that Jesus Himself drew near and went with them. But their eyes were restrained, so that they did not know Him. And He said to them, "What kind of conversation is this that you have with one another as you walk and are sad?" Then the one whose name was Cleopas answered and said to Him, "Are You the only stranger in Jerusalem, and have You not known the things which happened there in these days?" And He said to them, "What things?" So they said to Him, "The things concerning Jesus of Nazareth, who was a Prophet mighty in deed and word before God and all the people."

Luke 24:13–19

True revival is seeing Jesus. At this point in the story, the men begin to describe to Jesus the things that He had just done for them. As their journey continues, their eyes are opened, and they see Jesus. But it is necessary for us to understand the crucial point at which their eyes were opened. Remember, revival is seeing Jesus.

Then they drew near to the village where they were going, and He indicated that He would have gone farther. But they constrained Him, saying, "Abide with us, for it is toward evening, and the day is far spent." And He went in to stay with them. Now it came to pass, as He sat at the table with them, that He took bread, blessed and broke it, and gave it to them. Then their eyes were opened and they knew Him; and He vanished from their sight. And they said to one another, "Did not our heart burn within us while He talked with us on the road, and while He opened the Scriptures to us?" So they rose up that very hour and returned to Jerusalem, and found the eleven and those who were with them gathered together, saying, "The Lord is risen indeed, and has appeared to Simon!" And they told about the things that had happened on the road, and how He was known to them in the breaking of bread.

Luke 24:28–35

They walked with the very substance they lacked. It is important to know that Jesus rebuked them for being slow of heart and for unbelief.

Then He said to them, "O foolish ones, and slow of heart to believe in all that the prophets have spoken! Ought not the Christ to have suffered these things and to enter into His glory?" And beginning at Moses and all the Prophets, He expounded to them in all the Scriptures the things concerning Himself.

Luke 24:25–27

Due to a religious filter (form without power, appearance without substance, talk without walk, fanfare but no fire, excitement without authority), they lacked perception and discernment. They lacked trust in what God had said through the prophets, so their eyes were darkened and restrained from seeing and burning. One of the primary works of revival is to open spiritual eyes darkened by religion. There can be no revelation in the atmosphere of religion. The only answer is a collision with revival on the road to a burning place.

133

Their eyes were restrained. The Bible says that the eyes of these men remained blinded to Jesus *until* the breaking of the bread. This is the cruical point that you need to remember on your spiritual journey. They arrived at Emmaus, the Burning Place, and at that place, their eyes were opened at the breaking of the bread. You cannot burn *for* Him until you break bread *with* Him. The bread represents a face-to-face encounter with Jesus every day.

They knew facts about Jesus, which they were talking about right in front of Him. As He began to explain passages of Scripture, something began to break inside of their hearts. Even still, they didn't yet see Him. It wasn't until the moment of the breaking of the bread that the blindness was penetrated by the light of His presence, and they saw Him. The book of Job records a powerful statement that describes this phenomenon. "My ears had heard of you but now my eyes have seen you" (Job 42:5 NIV).

> You cannot burn **for** Him until you break bread **with** Him.

If you truly want personal and corporate revival, you must make it to the breaking of the bread. You must move past hearing only into the place of seeing Him. This happens in the burning place as you move past "have you heard what happened" and land in the moment of "now my eyes see You." That is the place of personal revival. You move past just talking about Him to walking with Him and seeing Him.

These men gave witness that they saw Jesus, and He was made known to them in the breaking of the bread. This is the moment when recognition becomes revelation. This was more than a natural meal; it was a supernatural reveal. Bread-breaking moments bring revelatory insight of Jesus.

Jesus uses a very ordinary moment to be a symbolic moment to reveal who He is. In the moment of the blessed and the broken, their eyes are opened to see and understand more of Him.

The Bread of Life was across the table from the doubters and the debaters who He met on the Road to Emmaus. Knowing that their eyes were blinded to who He was, He performed a miracle during the breaking of the bread. As they partook of the broken, blessed bread with Him, their eyes were opened to His revelation. That miracle opened their spiritual eyes and their understanding of who Jesus is. No longer would they only talk about Jesus—now their eyes could see Him. This is revival.

Bread-breaking moments are coming to hungry believers, revival moments of face-to-face encounters with Jesus who is walking into the burning place in their secret place in the Spirit. The Church will burn again as it was born to do. As the Church meets Jesus once again face to face, they will receive burning hearts that this world cannot deny.

Religion fights to keep us from these bread-breaking moments that lead to the fullness of revival. Remember, before we can burn, we must see Him. Between the spiritual blindness of verse 16 and the revelation of verse 31 was a bread-breaking moment. They saw Jesus in the burning place, and they burned. When we're on the road with Jesus, we should not ignore the burning moments because they're leading us to a bread-breaking moment in the burning place. We are to live in the burning place—not only the burning moments.

I pray for bread-breaking moments for you today. This is truly the supernatural substance that will sustain your personal spiritual revival. In the natural, bread is a filling substance. The same is true in the spiritual. He is the Bread of Life, the filling portion. The innate spiritual hunger placed by God within each of us can only be satisfied by His eternal presence. We will forever feast on Him, the opportunity to begin the feast now should not be ignored. We should long for bread-breaking moments so that we can burn for Him.

In the Old Testament Tabernacle, the Table of Shewbread was also called the Bread of His Presence. It was located right outside the Holy of Holies and signified the fullness of revival. In Hebrew, this table means "face bread or bread of faces."[1] It represented the intimacy of the fullness of God's Spirit found in His presence in the symbolism of His face. Revival is face bread. When did the men on the road to Emmaus see Jesus? When He broke bread. Jesus sat across the table with them and broke open His presence to them. He revealed who He was in an intimate moment. Sitting across the table from them, face-to-face, they saw Him for the first time. Before this moment, they had only heard of Him. Now their eyes saw Him.

God told Moses to make a table in His dwelling place or tabernacle. On this table, Moses was to place continual fresh bread. God told him that it was when he was standing before this bread that he would be standing facing His presence, face-to-face, continually.

The bread on this table was to be twelve fresh loaves every day. No leftovers, no stale bread. The price for providing fresh bread every day was costly, yet it speaks as to how fresh our encounter with Jesus should be. Just as the bread on the Table of Shewbread could not be stale, neither can your spiritual bread. You need a daily face-to-face encounter with Jesus, the Bread of Life, to live in a burning place. Don't forget that the bread was broken in the burning place. Don't stop walking, He's leading you into a burning place to break the bread so that you can see Him. Then you will burn!

It is worth noting that bread, not any other food, was the food of choice for this table. It represented Jesus, the Bread of Life, who said that He is the Bread sent down from heaven (see John 6:35). He said that He is the Face of God revealed. "For God, who said, 'Let there be light in the darkness,' has made this light shine in our hearts so we could know the glory of God that is seen in the face of Jesus Christ" (2 Corinthians 4:6 NLT).

There will be many distractions that try to keep you from making it to that table with Jesus. But the glory of God that is seen in His face will be worth all your time and sacrifice. You'll never regret seeing His face. You'll never forget seeing His face. And you'll never relent to see Him again and again. Bread-breaking moments are where you can say, "I can see You now."

Something happens when you walk with Jesus on the road. He will always lead you to a burning place in the Spirit. There He will break the bread of His presence with you, and at that moment, everything will change. You will burn. Those who are desperate live in the burning place. Let's now go explore another road called Damascus.

You'll never regret seeing His face.

A man named Saul collided with Jesus on Damascus Road. There, religion collided with revival. Like the men on the road to Emmaus whose eyes were blinded spiritually, Saul's spiritual eyes were also blinded; however, his natural eyes became blinded, too. This blinding happened due to the impact of the collision with the glory light found in Jesus. This was strategic so that he could begin to see in the Spirit, so that he could begin to burn for nations and open their blinded eyes to see Jesus as he did.

Locked up inside of this man were nations and revelations. But scales of religion had to be burned out by a collision with Jesus on the road to Damascus. "And he said, 'The God of our fathers has appointed you to know His will and to see the Righteous One and to hear an utterance from His mouth'" (Acts 22:14 NASB). Saul, who became Paul, was destined to see the Righteous One and hear revelation from His mouth. This is why Paul would later write, "I pray that the eyes of your heart may be enlightened so that you will know what is the hope of His calling, what are the riches of the glory of His inheritance in the saints" (Ephesians 1:18 NASB).

The eyes of our heart are where we burn. The two on the road to Emmaus recognized that their hearts did burn within them. The eyes in our heart should be enlightened or flooded with light by the Holy Spirit so that we can clearly see Him. The poet John Donne said, "God alone sees the heart; the heart alone sees God!"[2]

Glory brings an ability to see what religion blinds us to. Ananias laid his hands on Saul, and Saul regains his natural sight. The Bible tells us that scales fell from his eyes, literally. "Immediately there fell from his eyes something like scales, and he received his sight at once" (Acts 9:18). I have thought could this possibly have been an actual deliverance for Saul. He was a man driven by anger unto murder, but who rose and was baptized after the scales fell off.

Whatever was behind the scales, once the obedient revivalist laid his hands on Saul and the scales fell, Saul's name was changed. His godly identity was renewed, and he became the apostle Paul. Nations and revelations were unlocked. Because of this collision with Jesus, one-third of the New Testament was written, and the entire continent of Europe was opened. Paul answered the Macedonian call, which opened the continent of Asia to the Gospel of Jesus Christ. All of this happened because he could say, "My ears had heard of you but now my eyes have seen you" (Job 42:5 NIV).

Religion will have you sit stifled and stoic in church service after church service, satisfied and blinded. But if you ever meet Jesus on the road, you'll never be the same. Your eyes will be opened and the potential within you will be unlocked. You'll never look back to that old condition because now you can see Him!

When you see Him, you will burn for Him. It is important to note that it was the apostle Paul who wrote, "Be enthusiastic to serve the Lord, keeping your passion toward Him boiling hot!" (Romans 12:11 TPT). Remember, we're talking about the burning place. The place where you see Jesus and burn. Paul said that whatever we do, we must keep our passion toward Jesus boiling hot. For water to boil, the heat must be burning hot.

We cannot ignore that Jesus gave basically the same directive to the church of Laodicea. "I could wish you were cold or hot . . . because you are lukewarm, and neither cold nor hot, I will vomit you out of My mouth" (Revelation 3:15). He only gave us two choices: cold or hot. It is gripping to think that Jesus wants either extreme, even if it is cold. I guess at least cold isn't hypocritical or apathetic. Cold needs a resurrection, lukewarm needs a revival. Jesus prefers cold over lukewarm.

Apparently, the spiritual temperature of lukewarm is the most difficult heart to reach because it is comfortable. It seems evident Jesus doesn't want us spiritually comfortable. He wants us burning, sold out, zealous, and fervent. Keep your passion toward Him boiling hot.

I asked the Lord, "How do I know that I'm burning?" The Holy Spirit immediately said, *When I am all-consuming.*

Keep your passion toward Him boiling hot.

He's an all-consuming fire! You know you're burning and boiling when He is all-consuming in your life and your lifestyle.

Jesus has always intended for His Church to burn. Remember, the original mantle for His Church was fire. It sat upon them, enveloped them, and dwelt with them. They were a dwelling place for the fire of the Spirit, and they burned for Jesus. They had been marked because they had seen Jesus.

A mark can be a recognizable sign or expression that identifies something. The Lord gave me a message a few years ago entitled "Branded by Burning; A Mark Made by Burning." The message conveyed that we are branded by God as we are seared with His fiery presence. This fiery presence leaves a permanent mark, a recognizable sign or expression that identifies us as His and having been with Him. When people look at our life, they should see the mark of His presence. The mark that signifies the time spent close to His presence and His fire.

God has called us to burn for Him, to be His burning, fiery ones. The verse in Romans shared earlier is an exhortation that we are to intentionally take inventory of our spiritual burning. In that same verse, Paul gave us the measuring stick for our pursuit. As we read above, "Be enthusiastic to serve the Lord, keeping your passion toward him boiling hot! Radiate with the glow of the Holy Spirit and let him fill you with excitement as you serve him" (Romans 12:11 TPT). Enthusiastic, passionate, boiling hot, and radiating with the glow of the Holy Spirit. This is quite the standard, but it is entirely possible as we intentionally pursue the Spirit. The outcome will be burning.

The phrase *burning ones* has become a trendy word within revival circles. I do believe there are many burning ones. As with any spiritual experience, however, we must be careful that we don't just jump on the burning bandwagon to identify with it without paying the price of living as a burning one.

Fire is recognizable, you cannot hide it. If you're burning, your life will be affected. It will produce a spiritual heating element in your heart that drives you closer to Him and the things of His Kingdom. Burning is neither pretty nor comfortable. It has an effect on every part of your flesh. This passion is a driving force in your life for none other than Him and His presence. All else is peripheral and secondary. This fire that has touched your life has changed the landscape of your perspective, and now you are a burning one. Everything in your path gets touched by this fire.

A point to consider: There are those who burn, and then there are those who choose to just bake. The difference lies in the effect that the heat has on your life and the lives of others. A burning one will leave an indelible mark on a life, a situation, or an atmosphere. A burning one will change the temperature and the spiritual climate from cold to hot wherever they go. A baking one, however, is content with only a certain amount of heat in a controlled environment that is all about their comfort. Burning leaves a mark, while baking leaves a person in control of whatever spiritual temperature he or she prefers, comfortably settled, just nicely roasting.

Another way to say it is that there are those who come to the campfire and jump into the fire and let the fire jump onto them so that they can burn, while there are those who come to the campfire but only want to sit around it to get nicely warm. They don't jump into it; therefore, they are not burning ones. Are you a burning one, or are you a baking one?

John the Baptist, the forerunner for Jesus, made a powerful statement about Him. In the context of John rebuking the religious Pharisees, he said, "As for me, I baptize you with water for repentance, but He who is coming after me is mightier than I, and I am not fit to remove His sandals; He will baptize you with the Holy Spirit and fire" (Matthew 3:11 NASB).

In our pursuit to be baptized in the Spirit, let's make sure that we receive this baptism of fire. Stay close to the presence of God until you burn and yearn for Him. Linger. Tarry. Wait with faith knowing that you will leave that encounter with the radiation of His glory.

When you're marked by the fire of God, you can be confident that it will produce some kind of radical effect in your life. This fire forces you out of religion and sentimental Christianity and puts you in a posture that longs to change the climate around you. You will have an insatiable desire to help others burn as you do. Fire is contagious!

You will feel this fire in your inward man. Jeremiah said it was like fire shut up in his bones (see Jeremiah 20:9). You can *know about* God without feeling anything because that knowledge has to do with intellect. Knowledge alone produces death. But when you truly *know God*, you will feel Him. You cannot be a burning one for God and not feel His presence burning within. If you burn, you will feel it. If there's no feeling, then you're probably not burning. You must press close to the fire until you feel it touch your flesh, emotions, and mental processes. Until then, you will not burn.

When was the last time that you were touched by God to the point that you had to ask Him to hold back because you couldn't handle the overwhelming pressure of His presence? Have you ever experienced that? It's in this place that you are branded by burning. Revival is more than just sitting in church services; it is the fire sitting in you. It is the place where you are seared by God to the point that His presence burns flesh and carnal desires and ignites a boiling hot flame of passion for Him. Everything in life is radically altered because you are a burning one.

To be branded is to have a mark made by burning. Remember, it is only in the burning that we can be marked. A good illustration would be the branding of livestock. Ranchers give their cattle a specific mark that represents their ranch so that their cattle can be easily identified as theirs. This mark will last the animal's lifespan. Traditionally and historically, this mark is made with metal heated in the fire.

This can easily be transferred into a spiritual setting. When we're marked by the fire of God, we are branded with the character of our Owner, and our home, heaven, becomes our identifying motivation. This is the power of being branded by burning.

Moses had the same thought in mind when He told God not to send them any further in their journey unless His mark went with them. He reminded God that the mark of His presence was going to be the identifying factor between the nation of Israel and other nations.

> Then he said to Him, "If Your presence does not go with us, do not lead us up from here. For how then can it be known that I have found favor in Your sight, I and Your people? Is it not by Your going with us, so that we, I and Your people, may be distinguished from all the other people who are upon the face of the earth?"
>
> Exodus 33:15–16 NASB

The early apostles had the mark of Jesus that spoke louder than their lack of education, as stated by the Pharisees, their number one antagonist.

> The council members were astonished as they witnessed the bold courage of Peter and John, especially when they discovered that they were just ordinary men who had never had religious training. Then they began to understand the effect [mark] Jesus had on them simply by spending time with him.
>
> Acts 4:13–14 TPT

Peter and John had an identifying mark that spoke to the religious and to the sinner, and it was that they had been with Jesus. Time with Jesus will mark you. I think it is important to note that they didn't have to market themselves because they were marked by the fire of God. If you burn, you will be noticed.

Consider that the modern definition of branding in the Church has become promotion for recognition. The traditional definition of branding, however, is pressure for identification. The first is to be noticed, the latter is that with which to associate. A *marked* difference! Promotion or pressure? So many are choosing promotion.

If you want to be a burning one, you must be seared in the secret place. To be seared is to burn the surface with a branding iron to expose the deeper flesh. There are many who will gather around the campfire because they like the feeling of the fire, the presence of the fire, the sounds of the fire, the warmth of the fire, yet they don't have a personal fireplace. The *corporate campfire* reflects our *personal fireplaces*.

Your spiritual personal fireplace is your secret place with Jesus. Can people say that you've been with Him? When you've been with Him, you will leave with a mark, His brand. People will not have to ask to whom you belong. They won't wonder who your Lord is, or if you are a Christian. No, they will be able to tell because the mark makes an indelible imprint. You will have received the mark made by pressure. You will have been seared in the secret place with Jesus. You burn for His person and for His purposes. You're branded by burning.

To maintain the intensity of the fire in your heart, your heart must constantly be stoked in the secret place by your personal spiritual fireplace with Jesus. Ask the Lord for a spirit of burning. "When the Lord has washed away the filth of the daughters of Zion, and purged the blood of Jerusalem from her midst, by the spirit of judgment and by the spirit of burning" (Isaiah 4:4).

The spirit of burning continuously abides within and cleanses and purges. It is the ignition element for the fire of God. This spirit of burning is what you meet at your personal fireplace. You're set ablaze as you gaze upon His fiery eyes and presence. Burning is more than a mental assent that comes with a moderate talk and casual encounter—it is yielding. Yield isn't a popular word because to yield is to give up one's rights and preferences. It involves surrendering and submitting. When someone yields, they must come under complete control of the Spirit of God.

It takes more than a mental assent and a casual decision to burn. It also takes more than agreeing with everything written in this chapter. You can agree and still not burn. To burn, you must give way to an all-consuming yielding of self. Real hunger for Him creates a capacity for Him. The reason we do not burn is because we're not hungry for it. The cry of want is access to the fire.

God, send us a baptism of fire today. May we burn for Your person and Your purpose. "I have come to set the earth on fire, and how I wish it were already ablaze with fiery passion for God!" (Luke 12:49 TPT).

TEN

Deep Calls unto Deep

The Lord spoke to me in one of our church's revival services and said, "You have tapped another well." It is not necessary to elaborate on the art or facts of well-digging to understand that if you dig and find water, you have dug deep enough below the surface to access it. Personal revival and spiritual pursuit require that you know how to dig. Spiritual well-diggers are not satisfied with surface or artificial means of spiritual hydration. They will dig until they find water. Deep calls unto deep! "Deep calls to deep at the sound of Your waterfalls; all Your breakers and Your waves have passed over me" (Psalm 42:7 NASB).

Just as Jesus told the Samaritan woman at the well about the living water, He let her glimpse into the deep of living water (see John 4:10–15). She responded, and her response led her into realms of the depth of God found in Christ she didn't know existed. This can happen for those who tap another well.

The Hebrew word for *deep* is *tehom*, and it means "sub-terranean waters," "an overwhelming sea," or "the abyss of the sea."[1] When we reach for God, we've reached for an unending, overwhelming presence. My desire is that this will propel you to greater depths and intensity in your spiritual pursuit.

There is a place in the Spirit where our deep meets God's deep. To go deep or achieve depth is to extend far down from the surface. This process speaks of the extent that we will go to reach deeper. As we call out from the place of our deep *need* for Him or our deep *desire* for Him, God answers from a place of deep love, power, presence, deliverance, and peace. Deep calls unto deep. As you dig deeper, you will achieve greater depth of understanding of who He is and what He is capable of. This is such a powerful motivation along our spiritual pursuit.

There is a deep well of deep deliverance and freedom in God. There is a deep well of deep relationship and encounter in God. We are given free access to both through the blood of Jesus Christ. It's time to start calling out to the deep of God. I must emphasize deep calls. A call means that there is a beckoning, an asking with authority that comes *from* heaven and is reciprocated by our beckoning and asking with authority *to* heaven. Deep calls unto deep.

It's time to start calling out to the deep of God.

The picture created is of deep deliverance, deep communion, and encounter. "In the same way the Spirit also helps our weakness; for we do not know how to pray as we should, but the Spirit Himself intercedes for us with groanings too deep for words" (Romans 8:26 NASB). Have you reached a place too deep for words lately? This verse paints a picture of deep deliverance and deep desire for God.

To sustain personal revival, you will want to continually call out to the deep. You must sustain dissatisfaction with superficial deliverance and surface relationships as these will be key factors to being an overcomer in the end times. Surface Christianity will not sustain you in the warfare that is ahead of you before Jesus returns. Jesus takes time to describe the seven churches of the End Time (see Revelation 2–3). A commonality was: *persecution and perseverance.*

What's going on in the Spirit? That is the question we should be asking right now as we see an atmosphere of chaos in the nations. These signs are indications of end times. Make sure that you have a grip on that spiritual reality as much as you do natural facts. We are being tested in our faith as never before, and the test is one of spiritual endurance and perseverance, the ability to endure a difficult process or situation without giving way. It means the capacity to last or withstand wear and tear. It is defined by durability, stability, longevity, resolution, and determination. We need all of these in this hour of our world. If we've not tapped into the deep in the Spirit, we will be overwhelmed in the natural. This is why it is imperative that we learn to call to the deep of God.

It would be just like an Antichrist spirit to have the Church spend two or three decades producing and reproducing shallow saints knowing that these people could not begin to make it through the warfare that is happening and is coming upon the earth. You might say that you believe in the rapture of the Church. So do I, but that doesn't mean that we will not have to endure a level of tribulation. No one has completely figured it out.

What do I do? Go deep! Deep calls unto deep. The only sustaining power that can keep us and empower us is found in the deep.

Unfortunately, some think that the meaning of deep is that they know more than anyone and are better than everyone. This is not deep; this is demonic pride. True deep takes us to a place of humility. The more hits we take and the more levels we reach, the more dependent we are on the depths of God. What we lack will become more apparent in the deep. Our deficit will be our downfall in the depths of the Spirit.

It is a fact of deep-sea diving that there is a depth of the ocean's pressure that can crush the human body.[2] This explains why only a few risk their life to go deeper into the ocean while the majority swim safely, playfully, and comfortably on the surface.

Going deep in the Spirit puts pressure on your flesh that is not on the surface. And this is why many swim in the shallow end. Shallow church has discipled thousands upon thousands of people to swim in the shallow end, and the byproduct is that shallow produces shallow. As the End Time warfare ramps up, those who have stayed shallow will have their spiritual deficit exposed. Possibly we will see casualties of people who neglected the deep.

As I type this chapter of the book, I am located at a wonderful ocean-front area. When I look out over my hotel balcony, I see the expanse of the Atlantic Ocean. As far as I can see, I notice the water. The farther away from shore one travels, the deeper the water becomes. Therein lies a lesson for us on our spiritual pursuit. The farther we go, the deeper we go. This is why we can never stop. As we go into our secret place with the Lord, we sit before an endless ocean of God's presence and power. And the farther we go into that presence, the deeper we go in Him. This is a key reality that we must keep in our hearts regardless of the swirl around us. He has us in His deep.

Psalm 42 was written at a time of great distress and affliction in David's life. Deep calls unto deep was a cry for deep deliverance and deep encounter. Many times, if not all times, great purpose and assignment is surrounded by deep distress, which is followed by a deep desire that has a depth of a cry that taps into a depth of God that others do not reach.

None of us ask for distress, but we know it will come. But it will also develop within us a cry for deep deliverance. Without it, we would swim on the surface unchallenged and unchanged. Deep desire is something that is cultivated. It is a choice that is to be cultivated. It is a cultivated cry for deeper than what we have and where we are. This is what it means to cry, deep unto deep. With this said, let's look at the depth of pain and warfare David expressed.

> Why are you in despair, my soul?
> And why are you restless within me?
> Wait for God, for I will again praise Him
> For the help of His presence, my God.
> My soul is in despair within me;
> Therefore I remember You from the land of the
>   Jordan
> And the peaks of Hermon, from Mount Mizar.
> Deep calls to deep at the sound of Your waterfalls;

151

All Your breakers and Your waves have passed over me.

Psalm 42:5–7 NASB2020

As David wrote this psalm, his soul was in despair. Warfare surrounded him, and he had reached a place of being overwhelmed. David's life was a constant battle. If it wasn't Saul, it was the Philistines. If it wasn't the Philistines, it was Michael. Then there was Absalom and other close friends who betrayed him. Yet this man was a man after God's own heart, and he was chosen and anointed as king. His kingship did not disqualify him for warfare. David spent a part of his life hiding, running, and weeping, but he never quit, and he never left God. He cried out as a soul in despair—deep calls unto deep. We are told how David strengthened himself in the Lord, and calling to the deep of God was one way that he did so (see 1 Samuel 30:6).

Deep desire is something that is cultivated.

Possibly this describes your life. Maybe not the same storyline, but the same warfare. If you've gotten knocked down by life or by the devil, understand that you have within you the ability to call out to the deep of God for a deep deliverance. You will be able to say to those around you who never thought you would rise again, "You watched me get knocked down. But stick around and watch how I get back up!" "For a righteous person falls seven times and rises again" (Proverbs 24:16 NASB2020).

Something I've learned after forty years of ministry is that we should look for and trust those who don't just watch us fall but who stay long enough to help us get back up. These are the ones who understand warfare and perseverance. The others just judge, criticize, and secretly rejoice at our pain.

Because you carry great purpose and great glory, you're guaranteed to navigate difficult seasons. If you live long enough, you'll hit up against it. The battle is for your purpose, peace, passion, position in authority, and spiritual fight. If the devil can steal any of these, he can keep you down. This is where you learn the call to the deep. Don't despair—there is deep deliverance waiting!

Jesus told us that we would have these times of affliction and despair in this world. "These things I have spoken to you, that in Me you may have peace. In the world you will have tribulation; but be of good cheer, I have overcome the world" (John 16:33). Joy is a choice during these times. It is not a feeling—it is a Fruit of the Spirit. It isn't natural, but supernatural. The Greek word for tribulation is *thlipsis* and it means "persecution, affliction, distress, or trouble."[3]

While none of us want any of this, we can count on it. Trouble will come. Jesus said it would. We live in a fallen world with an adversary, the devil, who is bent on keeping us from our God-assignment. But on the inside of the child of God is God's DNA, and that DNA contains the same overcoming Spirit that Jesus possessed. To be an overcomer means that you exercise controlling influence *over* the circumstance. Apostle Paul gives us a glimpse into what this looks like. "We are hard-pressed on every side, yet not crushed; we are perplexed, but not in despair; persecuted, but not forsaken; struck down, but not destroyed" (2 Corinthians 4:8–9). And then he says, "Who shall separate us from the love of Christ? Shall tribulation, or distress, or persecution, or famine, or nakedness, or peril, or sword? Yet *in* all these things we are more than conquerors through Him who loved us" (Romans 8:35–37).

In or amid all the circumstances, we can exercise controlling influence. When we do, we overcome. There is not a weapon or strategy that the devil has that can take us out. Even if we were to taste death, the other side is eternal life. We win no matter what. We win!

Joyce Meyer wrote, "We can't control what other people do and how they decide to treat us, but we can control our response to them."[4] Having never forgotten this powerful statement, I have looked at every challenge through this lens. If you refuse to get underneath the warfare, you cannot be overcome by it. Go deeper. Deep pain, deeper deliverance. Exercise controlling influence and authority no matter what may come your way.

We are assured that everything is working according to God's design and purpose. "We are assured and know that [God being a partner in their labor] all things work together and are [fitting into a plan] for good to and for those who love God and are called according to [His] design and purpose" (Romans 8:28 AMPC). The warfare will *never* stop, which is why we must go deep. We will not stop, either!

Deep pain, deeper deliverance.

"Let's hold firmly to the confession of our hope without wavering, for He who promised is faithful" (Hebrews 10:23 NASB).

Life and death are in the power of the tongue (see Proverbs 18:21). So watch your spoken words during these times, keep your confession of faith, keep the Word of God on your lips and in your heart, and then be careful to listen to the words of those around you. Begin to align yourself with those who can help you see past your pain to remember your purpose. Your voice matters, and it shatters the powers of darkness. You want to arm yourself and surround yourself with words that break through. It is in these pressing times that you launch out into the deep. From the place of the deep, you draw on deep strength and resolve that is only found in the depths of God that will carry and deliver you.

I would love to help lead you to a place of purpose in your spiritual pursuit. Every pain that you have encountered is leading you to your place of purpose. Begin to lift the authority of the Lord. The power of God, the victory of God, the authority of God, and the love and mercy of God. Begin to declare the names of God:

El-Shaddai—God Almighty
Adonai—Lord and Master
Jireh—Provider
Rapha—Healer
Shalom—Peace
Rohi—Shepherd
Shammah—He Who Never Leaves or Forsakes Me
Sabaoth—Lord of Hosts
Gmolah—God of Recompense, God Who Will Repay
Nissi—My Victory, Banner, and Standard.

The name of the Lord is my battle cry. You are my God who prevails! Call on these names of God and watch how the enemy scatters. There is power in His name. "May God arise, may His enemies be scattered, and may those who hate Him flee from His presence" (Psalm 68:1 NASB2020).

Begin to call out to the deep this powerful revival verse found in the book of Isaiah.

> Oh, that You would rend the heavens and come
>   down,
> That the mountains would quake at Your presence—
> As fire kindles the brushwood, as fire causes water to
>   boil—
> To make Your name known to Your adversaries,
> That the nations may tremble at Your presence!
> When You did awesome things which we did not
>   expect,
> You came down, the mountains quaked at Your
>   presence.
> For from days of old they have not heard or
>   perceived by ear,
> Nor has the eye seen a God besides You,
> Who acts in behalf of one who waits for Him.
>
> Isaiah 64:1–4 NASB

The deep of the presence and power of God causes all adversaries to quake and shake. And never forget, the devil is no match for the God in us. His method of operation is easy to detect. It will always be counterfeit, confusion, deception, evil, wickedness, manipulation, control, fear, and lies.

Everything that the early Christians accomplished for Christ was surrounded by warfare. Whether an early Christian was an apostle, deacon, or follower of the newly formed Way, he or she encountered intense tribulation all around. We must find ourselves in the same posture and attitude of these early believers if we are to finish what they began. I

encourage you to go deep. Hear the words of the apostle
Paul. Follow him as he followed Christ.

> Yet, as God's servants, we prove ourselves authentic in every
> way. For example: We have great endurance in hardships and
> in persecutions. We don't lose courage in a time of stress
> and calamity. We've been beaten many times, imprisoned,
> and found ourselves in the midst of riots. We've endured
> many troubles, had sleepless nights, and gone hungry. We
> have proved ourselves by our lifestyles of purity, by our
> spiritual insights, by our patience, and by showing kind-
> ness, by the Spirit of holiness and by our uncritical love
> for you. We commend ourselves to you by our truthful
> teachings, by the power of God working through us, and
> with the mighty weapons of righteousness—a sword in one
> hand and a shield in the other. Amid honor or dishonor,
> slander or praise—even when we are treated as deceivers
> and imposters—we remain steadfast and true. We are un-
> known nobodies whom everyone knows. We are frequently
> at death's door, yet here we are, still alive! We have been
> severely punished yet not executed. We may suffer, yet in
> every season we are always found rejoicing. We may be poor,
> yet we bestow great riches on many. We seem to have noth-
> ing, yet in reality we possess all things.
>
> 2 Corinthians 6:4–10 TPT

We turn now to the depth of pursuit and longing. "As the
deer pants for the water brooks, so my soul pants for You,
O God. My soul thirsts for God, for the living God" (Psalm
42:1–2 NASB). The depth of His divine presence calls for a
deeper depth of longing within us. As the deer longs for the
water, our soul should long for the deep. Deep calls unto

deep. The following verse is a powerful picture of spiritual longing. "I long to drink of you, O God, to drink deeply from the streams of pleasure flowing from your presence. My longings overwhelm me for more of you" (Psalm 42:1–2 TPT).

To say that the bottom line of personal revival is continual longing for the more of Him sounds trivial to some. Some want evidence of supernatural manifestations and reports of resounding sermons of repentance and victory. These are an integral part of revival, but as we've said, the deeper we go, the more we'll encounter supernatural inclination to more. Deep calls unto deep! The deeper we go in Him, the more we crave Him. Trying to make revival about anything less than a ravenous pursuit of the depths of God is like taking a life-giving substance away from a starving child. His presence is everything, and because He dwells in the deep, there is always more.

To stay in God's presence is like being immersed in the ocean. It is a never-ending encounter of more. "The ancient depths surge" (Psalm 42:7 THE VOICE). This is a powerful picture of what it is like as we go deeper with God. The description of ancient depths is breathtaking. For all eternity—what has been and what is to come—we can swim in the depths of God and never run out of more of Him. The depths are surging. They're waiting on someone to overtake and overwhelm them. This is revival. This is the power of calling out to the depths of God. You have full permission to go deep. Pursue Him. There is more.

I'm urging you today to go past mental assent and past protocol that has been learned. Go to a place in the deep where the ancient depths are surging and you are out of control. Go to a place where you get lost in your human understanding and relinquish to Him so much that His deep connects with a deep cry within you. Can you go there? His abiding presence is undeniably precious, but His manifested presence means that you have dug until you have tapped out of this realm and into His. Deep calls unto deep.

ELEVEN

The Stairway of Ascent

In the last chapter, we talked about going deeper. Let's talk about going higher. Deeper and higher are accurate spiritual terms that describe our spiritual pursuit. To dive deeper means being grounded and rooted spiritually, and going higher spiritually takes us closer and into greater intimacy with God than where we are presently. From the book of Ezekiel and the book of Psalms, we will look at what I call the stairway of ascent. These are levels used to climb into greater relationship with the Lord.

> "But the Levitical priests, the sons of Zadok, who took responsibility for My sanctuary when the sons of Israel went astray from Me, shall come near to Me to serve Me; and they shall stand before Me to offer Me the fat and the blood," declares the Lord GOD. "They shall enter My sanctuary; they shall come near to My table to serve to Me and assume the responsibility I give them."
>
> Ezekiel 44:15–16 NASB2020

But continue to grow and increase in God's grace and intimacy with our Lord and Savior, Jesus Christ.

2 Peter 3:18 TPT

But the love of God will be perfected within the one who obeys God's Word. We can be sure that we've truly come to live in intimacy with God, not just by saying, "I am intimate with God," but by walking in the footsteps of Jesus.

1 John 2:5–6 TPT

Within your spirit as a born-again believer and a Spirit-filled revivalist is a *stairway of ascent*, or a means of access to higher levels and degrees of the presence of God and the revelation of God. The more you give yourself to this pilgrimage, this journey or pursuit, the closer you get to God and His manifested presence. And the closer you get to His presence, the more He reveals of Himself.

The secret is in the climb. No one can climb for you. In the last days, you'll not be able to sustain a victorious, intimate Christian walk on secondhand revelation. You must make your own climb. You have your own homework to do. This is not something that you can delegate or dismiss—you must make this climb.

These stairs give access to greater degrees of spiritual maturity from the presence of God. My prayer is that the Body of Christ becomes stair-climbing revivalists. I hope making every effort to continuously climb the stairway of ascent becomes your passion.

You must make your own climb.

This is what I call *the discipline of desperation.* This is a posture of the heart that says, "No matter what, I will remain in a heart posture of urgent, extreme, excessive desire for Jesus." This will cultivate a hungry ache within to see Jesus, His power, and His glory. It produces an evident depth of spiritual substance and a deepened spiritual capacity. Your next level in the Spirit is born out of a decision to take another step higher.

> Brothers and sisters, I do not regard myself as having taken hold of it yet; but one thing I do: forgetting what lies behind and reaching forward to what lies ahead, I press on toward the goal for the prize of the upward call of God in Christ Jesus.
>
> Philippians 3:13–14 NASB2020

Pressing implies pursuing, moving, and making forward or upward progress. It is a pilgrimage. Pressing forward is a powerful force because it indicates action and annihilates stagnancy.

You cannot take a step upward on the stairway of ascent while focusing on what is behind you. You cannot grab the next step with God while holding onto an old wineskin or encounter. I press forward to take hold of the prize of the upward call (see Philippians 4:13). It is an upward call, indicating it is a climb.

Your time spent climbing locates the level of spiritual pursuit. The fruit of our lives speaks and displays our current level of pursuit. Is this important? Apparently so!

> But seek (aim at and strive after) first of all His kingdom and His righteousness (His way of doing and being right), and then all these things taken together will be given you besides.
>
> Matthew 6:33 AMPC

163

Your pursuit is what you'll be passionate about. And while our natural life demands a pursuit of certain things to create a livelihood and take care of our families, this pursuit and other natural pursuits should not create a substitute passion that is greater than our passionate pursuit for Jesus and His presence. Again, the word *pursuit* defined is "to crave, go after with all your strength, to sacrifice other things, require as a vital necessity in life; to seek for." "And without faith living within us it would be impossible to please God. For we come to God in faith knowing that he is real and that he rewards the faith of those who passionately seek him" (Hebrews 11:6 TPT).

God rewards passionate seekers! Passionate pursuit makes the difference. Apparently, maintaining a fiery first love is important to Jesus. He took time to point this out in the book of Revelation. To have a *passive* pursuit also makes a difference as we see in Jesus' rebuke to the church of Ephesus.

> But I have this against you: you have abandoned the passionate love you had for me at the beginning. Think about how far you have fallen! Repent and do the works of love you did at first. I will come to you and remove your lampstand from its place of influence if you do not repent.
>
> Revelation 2:4–5 TPT

I want to motivate you for the climb. It gets steep and it gets hard, but the reward is worth it. Let these verses motivate and inspire you for the climb.

> YAHWEH, who dares to dwell with you? Who presumes the privilege of being close to you, living next to you in your

shining place of glory? They are passionate and whole-hearted, always sincere and always speaking the truth—for their hearts are trustworthy.

Psalm 15:1–2 TPT

Listen to me, all you godly ones: Love the Lord with passion! The Lord protects and preserves all those who are loyal to him. But he pays back in full all those who reject him in their pride.

Psalm 31:23 TPT

Give me an understanding heart so that I can passionately know and obey your truth.

Psalm 119:34 TPT

Passion's birthplace is in intimacy. Intimacy levels can be judged by passion levels. If you are passionate about something, you'll choose intimacy, in which intimacy is defined as close association and affection with another, detailed knowledge of the other, and deep understanding of someone. The devil is after your passion. The enemy is deploying deception into the Church like never before. This strategy is directed at enticing God's people away from moving into the higher realms in God and intimacy with the Father. I'm concerned that End Time warfare will take people out who haven't cultivated a passionate intimacy with the Lord. Anything less is surface and can be easily breached. Only an intimate relationship with Jesus can withstand End Time, demonic warfare.

The End Time warfare will be intense because the devil already knows his fate. He hates you and me because we are the image of Jesus Christ. We remind him of what he gave up. We carry the essence of the heavenly realm within us, and it frustrates him because he can never achieve that. The atmosphere and majesty that he rebelled against is what

Passion's birthplace is in intimacy.

blood-bought believers carry within their spirits. The devil knows that if we ever get our passions aligned with eternity, we can climb the stairway of ascent into realms and regions of God's glory that only the angelic and those who have passed on before us have known. His plan of action, therefore, is to steal our passion!

The devil will allow you to keep doing all the stuff that Christians do, which was the picture of Ephesus. He understands that passion is what leads to devotion, so he will try to steal your passion. If your spiritual pursuit is for any other reason than for God and God alone, your devotion, profound dedication, consecration, and zeal for Him will be short-lived.

Devotion goes beyond service—it leads to sacrifice. And until we are awakened to who He is and not just what He does, we will remain at shallow levels of devotion. But when our eyes are opened to His holiness, purity, and majesty, nothing will keep us from the continual pursuit of Him. We will be on a pilgrimage to ascend the stairway to more.

At some point in our pursuit, the attraction to the lesser must go. This will only happen if we take steps higher on the stairway of ascent drawing closer and closer to Him. I remember this incredible hymn I sang as a child in church:

> Turn your eyes upon Jesus
> Look full in His wonderful face

And the things of earth will grow strangely dim
In the light of His glory and grace.[1]

Charles Spurgeon, the highly influential and prolific British preacher from the 1800s said, "Nothing teaches us about the preciousness of the Creator as much as when we learn the emptiness of everything else."[2]

When spiritual passion begins to wane, we cannot continue as though it has not. If that happens, we have left revival. We must stop and assess our place on the spiritual climb. We must confess our lack of zeal and our stalled pursuit and begin to take another step into the pursuit of His holiness and beauty. When we live from a view of eternity, the temporal will bore us. Until we have revelation that the only thing that matters in this life and the next is our progressive pursuit of Jesus, we will maintain a status quo pursuit of God.

At the same time, competing temporal goals will consume and waste our passions on this earth. To avoid this, we must have a discipline of desperation to make the climb. "So live the rest of your earthly life no longer concerned with human desires but consumed with what brings pleasure to God" (1 Peter 4:2 TPT). The deeper your desperation, the more of your lesser life must be released. This is a line that defines the hard-core pursuer. The greater weight of His glory must become more important than the temporal bait.

Why would you choose the lesser? It's time to ascend. I want to instill in us a conviction to continually climb. Climbing takes effort. There are rewards for those who have a climbing conviction. He rewards those who passionately seek Him (see Hebrews 11:6). The spiritual climb creates a spiritual capacity that can carry greater spiritual weight. And if revival is going to be sustained, this is a conviction that cannot be ignored.

Psalms 120–134 are collectively known as A Song of the Stairway. It is believed that possibly these fifteen songs were sung on the fifteen steps that would take the Jewish worshiper into Solomon's temple. On each step they would stop to worship and sing the corresponding psalm as they went up higher into the worship of God.

They were also known as Pilgrim Songs. Three times a year, the Hebrew people were to take a pilgrimage or pursuit to Jerusalem to worship the Lord (see Deuteronomy 16:16; Luke 2:41). These pilgrims or pursuers would ascend these stairs to enter the temple to worship.

It is a fact that the steps, also known as the Southern Steps, were uneven. They were purposely built that way to make people think about the upward climb into His presence. A person can't run up the stairs into His presence without thinking about each step intentionally. There was a purposeful contemplation of the ascent into the presence of God.

Some have made church so casual that it is easy to forget what and Who they are approaching. I'm not for dead, dry formalism that has no Holy Ghost on it, but I do believe that our casual and familiar thought processes have moved us downward in reverence. We should be ascending upward into the awe of His holiness. Beware of those who have nice, evenly laid steps in their pursuit!

The steps of a righteous man are ordered of the Lord (see Psalm 37:23). His order is higher than our ordering.

He knows right where to place a step in the ascent that will stretch our stride and lengthen our lunge in the spirit.

Just when we think we've got this ascent figured out, here comes a long step where we have to wait to learn a level of worship we've not been to before. Then the next will be a shorter, narrower step to teach us faith to move upward to another level with spiritual caution and accuracy. Solomon modeled this reverence for us.

We should be ascending upward into the awe of His holiness.

> When the queen of Sheba perceived all the wisdom of Solomon, the house that he had built, the food of his table, the seating of his servants, the attendance of his waiters and their attire, his cupbearers, and his stairway by which he went up to the house of the LORD [the King James Version uses the word *ascent*], there was no more spirit in her.
>
> 1 Kings 10:4–5 NASB

This pagan, heathen queen came to visit Solomon, and she was speechless and breathless at the reverential, passionate protocol of King Solomon as he sacrificed, worshiped, and ascended into the house of the Lord. When our reverence for presence exceeds our need for comfort, convenience, and popularity we will prioritize the ascent of the spiritual stairway of intimate pursuit.

There was a man in the Bible named Zadok. He was a priest who had to make choices that went against his flesh and his reputation. But in the end, he and his entire lineage were rewarded with a special place of nearness to the presence of God. In the book of Ezekiel, the sons of Zadok were given greater access and relationship with the Lord than others.

> "But the Levites who went far from Me when Israel went astray, who went astray from Me after their idols, shall bear the punishment for their iniquity. Yet they shall be ministers in My sanctuary. . . . They shall not come near to Me to serve as a priest to Me, nor come near to any of My holy things, to the things that are most holy; but they will bear their shame and their abominations which they have committed. . . .
>
> "But the Levitical priests, the sons of Zadok, who kept charge of My sanctuary when the sons of Israel went astray from Me, shall come near to Me to minister to Me; and they shall stand before Me to offer Me the fat and the blood," declares the Lord GOD. "They shall enter My sanctuary; they shall come near to My table to minister to Me and keep My charge."
>
> Ezekiel 44:10–16 NASB

> "Moreover, they shall teach My people the difference between the holy and the profane, and cause them to discern between the unclean and the clean. In a dispute they shall take their stand to judge; they shall judge it according to My ordinances. They shall also keep My laws and My statutes in all My appointed feasts and sanctify My sabbaths."
>
> Ezekiel 44:23–24 NASB

There were certain Levitical priests who were not allowed in the manifest presence of God. They were limited to the outer courts of God's presence. But the sons of Zadok were given access to higher places in the physical temple and in spiritual authority. They were given access to the manifest presence of God and the higher purposes of God, and here's why.

Zadok was the high priest during David's reign. When all of Israel went astray and followed Absalom, Zadok, at David's instruction, picked up the Ark and followed David even though it seemed that action would mean certain doom. Zadok did not do what was popular, he did what was right. He knew that the Lord had anointed David and not Absalom. David was still king, even though all Israel did not see it that way. The crowd paid a dear price, which was distance from God's presence, but Zadok's reward would last forever. To this day, his spiritual sons are those who are closest to the Lord, those who follow the presence at all costs.

For a long time, Zadok was co-high priest with Abiathar. Zadok and Abiathar heard that Absalom planned to seek out David and destroy him and the people who were with him. David escaped, but it wasn't much longer before David's commander, Joab, killed Absalom. Heartbroken at the death of his son, David returned to Jerusalem. Years later, when King David was very old, his son Adonijah set himself up as king, even though David's other son Solomon was to take the throne at David's death. Adonijah had some followers, including Abiathar the priest, but Zadok supported David's choice and opposed Adonijah. David ordered Zadok and Nathan to immediately take Solomon and anoint him king.

Zadok stayed true to David and supported Solomon. Abiathar lost his priesthood because of his betrayal, but Zadok was rewarded with a position as one of Solomon's chief officials, as well as being recognized as the sole high priest. Both of these men, Zadok and Abiathar, had fruitful ministries but both faced decisions that would determine the rest of their lives. The consequences of the decision of both Zadok and Abiathar were far reaching in their lives and their descendants' lives.

Zadok, along with his descendants, found such important favor with God that it was worthy of mention in God's Word, and it is used as an example to us all. Zadok chose the pursuit, Abiathar chose popularity. Throughout David's life, Zadok always stayed with him because he knew where God was. If God had left David, he would have, too, it seems.

Zadok was made the chief priest (see 1 Kings 2:35). That was a wonderful job, giving him the opportunity to serve right beside David. Before this, Abiathar had that job, but had to be removed from it. Zadok was loyal; therefore, he was given the chief seat and the authority to direct all the ministers. He was a priest's priest because he was loyal to David and to God from beginning to end. You might have heard someone use the phrase *sons of Zadok* to describe the faithful people of God.

Not every example was perfect, but the Bible records some great deeds performed by the sons of Zadok anciently. And God bestowed additional honor on that faithful priest by attaching his name to an inspiring prophecy.

> "But the Levitical priests, the sons of Zadok, who kept charge of My sanctuary when the sons of Israel went astray from Me, shall come near to Me to minister to Me; and they shall stand before Me. . . . They shall enter My sanctuary;

they shall come near to My table to minister to Me and keep
My charge."

Ezekiel 44:15–16 NASB

Ezekiel talks about a chamber in that temple whose prospect is toward the north (see Ezekiel 40). That chamber is for the priests whom God calls the sons of Zadok among the sons of Levi. God declares that only the sons of Zadok are going to come near to Him. This is the honor that awaits the sons of Zadok today!

It is possible that the Holy Spirit was orchestrating the construction of the ascension steps into the temple during Zadok's time. He followed not only David but also Solomon, and Solomon built the steps that led into the temple.

Zadok didn't just stay with a man, He stayed with God's standard. Both David and Solomon were committed to building a habitation for God. Zadok was put in a position to choose the popular will of the people or the prophetic will of God from that time on and forever. By choosing the latter, Zadok was instrumental in preserving a dwelling place for God.

Sustained personal revival will take a people like Zadok who do not compromise the popular for the prophetic. A sustained presence requires a sustained standard if we're going to follow that which God has ordained.

Zadok didn't settle, and because of it, a place in history was reserved for that priestly line. They were granted sole rights to ascend the stairs and to dwell near the stairway, the place of ascension to God.

The side chambers surrounding the temple were wider at each successive story. Because the structure surrounding the temple went upward by stages on all sides of the temple, therefore the width of the temple increased as it went higher; and thus one went up from the lowest story to the highest by way of the second story [on a winding stairway].

Ezekiel 41:7 NASB

These stairs inside of the temple are in an area that was reserved for the Zadok priesthood only. They had exclusive rights to ascend because, in the difficult times, Zadok chose the presence of God. It's worthy to note that the physical structure of the temple got wider as it went higher. The higher you ascend, the greater the capacity of His presence.

The spirit of Absalom and Adonijah is still active in the earth today. It comes in different forms, but the goal of each spirit is to draw you away from the presence and protocol of God. To get you out of order and away from God's standard.

Adonijah's uprising was in direct opposition to the establishment of the stairway of ascent. He was rising to usurp David and take what rightfully belonged to Solomon who was directed by God Himself to build the stairway. But it takes a Zadok heart and determination to follow the presence, the ark, and David because he is following the presence. "My whole being follows hard after You" (Psalm 63:8 AMPC).

Within your spirit as a born-again believer and a Spirit-filled revivalist is a stairway of ascent or means of access to

174

higher levels and degrees of the presence of God and the revelation of God. The more you give yourself to this pilgrimage, journey, or pursuit, the closer you get to God and His manifested presence, and the more you uncover of Him.

The secret is in the climb. It's in the journey, and it's in the pursuit. You are one step away from more of God. Make the climb!

TWELVE

A Heart Set on a Pilgrimage

How lovely is your dwelling place, Lord Almighty! My soul yearns, even faints, for the courts of the Lord; my heart and my flesh cry out for the living God. Even the sparrow has found a home, and the swallow a nest for herself, where she may have her young—a place near your altar, Lord Almighty, my King, and my God. Blessed are those who dwell in your house; they are ever praising you. Blessed are those whose strength is in you, whose hearts are set on pilgrimage. As they pass through the Valley of Baka, they make it a place of springs; the autumn rains also cover it with pools. They go from strength to strength, till each appears before God in Zion. Hear my prayer, Lord God Almighty; listen to me, God of Jacob. Look on our shield, O God; look with favor on your anointed one. Better is one day in your courts than a thousand elsewhere; I would rather be a doorkeeper in the house of my God than dwell in the tents of the wicked.

Psalm 84:1–10 NIV

177

A pilgrimage is a journey to a sacred place. This precisely describes our spiritual pursuit. In the above psalm, the psalmist puts words to the beat of a heart set on a pilgrimage. The description is very intense because the longing is intense. My mind, will, and emotions yearn for the presence of God. My flesh cries out for God. Then he says that even the birds find a place at the altar of the Lord, and blessed is anyone who will dwell in His presence praising Him.

In the psalm, we see a gripping phrase that I want to highlight and trust that it will be the highlight of this book for you. "Blessed are those whose strength is in you, whose hearts are set on pilgrimage." Is your heart set on your journey to His presence? To have our heart set on something implies that we have a strong desire for it. If we do not get it or achieve it, we will experience great disappointment.

Several years ago, the Lord dropped the following phrase in my heart: the longing to long and the yearning to yearn. As a response, I prayed that He would give me a longing to long and a yearning to yearn. He wants us to cry out to Him in this manner. This type of prayer and those like it reveal a heart that is set on Him. It reveals desperation and longing that will not be denied.

I hope that you can feel the presence of the Lord around you as you read this. Blessed are those whose heart is set on a pilgrimage. Even as you go through the valley of weeping, which is another word for Baka, your heart is set. Because of this, you can go from strength to strength. It doesn't stop there. The verse continues by saying that just one day in His courts is better than a thousand in any other place. What you receive in His courts far outweighs what you can receive anywhere else. Is your heart set? You were born for this journey of worship to God.

> All has been heard; the end of the matter is: Fear God [revere and worship Him, knowing that He is] and keep His commandments, for this is the whole of man [the full, original purpose of his creation, the object of God's providence, the root of character, the foundation of all happiness, the adjustment to all inharmonious circumstances and conditions under the sun] and the whole [duty] for every man.
>
> Ecclesiastes 12:13 AMPC

According to Ecclesiastes, after all is said and done, every person will have the worship of God as their entire duty and responsibility. This was the purpose in the beginning, and it will be our purpose throughout eternity. While we may have a thousand other duties pulling on us right now, we were born for one thing—the worship of God. We were born to worship Him, and we were created for His pleasure.

Blessed are those whose heart is set on a pilgrimage.

Worship is a constant in heaven; therefore, the atmosphere of heaven produces the glory of God, and glory is the atmosphere of heaven. As revivalist and prayer warrior Ruth Heflin said, "As air is to the atmosphere of the earth, glory is the atmosphere of Heaven."[1] It is absolutely incredible to think that we can have this atmosphere of glory as we worship. Being enveloped in heaven's atmosphere is what keeps us focused on this pilgrimage.

The studies that I have done on heaven have confirmed that all who have had visions of heaven or who have died but have come back to talk about it have hinted that they heard constant music and worship in heaven. Should we be surprised that you will always hear worship in heaven? It cannot be heaven if it doesn't have worship of God. And I will add, we cannot experience heaven on earth if we do not have worship of God.

> I, John, saw and heard these things. And when I heard and saw, I fell down to worship before the feet of the angel who showed me these things. Then he said to me, "See that you do not do that. For I am your fellow servant, and of your brethren the prophets, and of those who keep the words of this book. *Worship God*."
>
> Revelation 22:8–9, emphasis added

Among the last words of the Bible are included the words *Worship God*. Worship is what we were created for. The worship of God is the end of all existence. One day, every part of creation will worship Him, even those who say they do not want to. We will all confess Jesus Christ as Lord and King. God created the universe so that it would display the worth of His glory, and He created us so that we would see this glory and reflect it by knowing and loving Him with all our heart, soul, mind, and strength.

Worship of God isn't only expressed through a song. It is a posture of the heart that honors the King just because He is King, He is Lord, and He is God. A heart that is set on a pilgrimage is a heart that is set on worship. You were born for this. I trust that phrase empowers you to set your heart. A quick personal story may help you grasp this better.

I was traveling for ministry with my husband. He doesn't always travel with me, but on this occasion, he chose to join me. We were at the rental car counter, and as the man was taking my information, he asked my birthdate. I told him what it was, and he very excitedly explained how I had been the third person he had encountered that day who had that birthdate. As I told my husband the story, his comment to me was, "You were born for this." He meant that I was born for the ministry to which I had been assigned on that trip.

> A heart that is set on a pilgrimage is a heart that is set on worship.

That was obviously an encouraging word for me, but what about my heart? What did that do for my heart? It helped me to set my heart to accomplish everything that was needed from me. It helped me realize that I had been equipped for everything that was going to be required from me. I hope that is what this chapter does for you. You were born for this pilgrimage. Set your heart on it.

True worship happens when it comes from a place in our heart where there is both revelation of Him and relationship with Him. This posture of our heart is what God longs for, true heart worship in spirit and in truth. We were created for this one purpose, and if we never become anything else, we can know that we will have fulfilled our highest purpose when we become worshipers. This should free us from any selfish ambition or false motivation. My highest honor is worship. My greatest calling is worship.

Jesus said to her, Woman, believe Me, a time is coming when you will worship the Father neither [merely] in this mountain

181

nor [merely] in Jerusalem. . . . A time will come, however, indeed it is already here, when the true (genuine) worshipers will worship the Father in spirit and in truth (reality); for the Father is seeking just such people as these as His worshipers.

John 4:21–23 AMPC

Jesus gave this woman one of the greatest revelations, because it reveals to us—straight from the mouth of Jesus, the Son of God—what God truly wants. He wants worshipers. Jesus points us to the posture of the heart. As our heart is set on a pilgrimage, a journey to the sacred place of His presence, our posture is deep worship from a place of spirit and truth. A longing to long, and a yearning to yearn. A never-ending heart posture that is set to worship Him.

David sustained true worship continually for 36 years during his kingship over Judah, and his order of worship is still in place today. What was that order of worship? It was a posture of heart that says: This is what I was born for, this is what it's all about, this is God's heart, and my heart is set on His heart, on a pilgrimage.

Your spiritual pilgrimage will bring a divine visitation that will become a divine habitation as you receive the revelation above all revelations, which is that the Father is seeking true worshipers and that you were born for this.

Trust me, this is the key to unlocking the next wave of personal revival. I can't give you a formula. I must, instead, lead you on a pilgrimage to a sacred place called a relationship. From that place of intimate relationship, you will develop awe and desperation that cannot be articulated with natural words and cannot be taken from you. No one will be able to stifle, steal, or sedate your worship. It will be uncontainable.

You will be undignified like David, undone like Isaiah, and will have an undeniable worship that magnifies the Lord like Mary.

As you set your heart on a pilgrimage, God will take you into the posture of heart that knows Him as the lover of your soul. There is a call to worship with a song of the heart that produces a sweet aroma to Him and opens the heavens. We need to pursue a path in which we fall in love with **You were born for this pilgrimage of worship.** Jesus so much that we are cautious and careful when we speak His name—that is how much awe we have of Him. From the place of the fear of the Lord, we cultivate a deep reverence and awe for Him.

A heart set on a pilgrimage is a sacred journey of worship with an attitude of the heart that bows before Him. There may be hundreds of people around you, but you are bowing to One. You were born for this pilgrimage of worship. His heart is set on it. I hope yours is, too.

I close this chapter and the book by giving a bit of the history of sustained revival at our church in Peoria, Arizona, Fresh Start Church. Through desperation to see God move, we began to seek the Lord for a marking measure of His presence to visit us. For about two years, we used our personal time and corporate time to deeply cultivate hearts of desperation and longing for God to manifest in greater measure. Our cry became, "Lord, come without measure!" He came. In August of 2015, we received our marking measure of His presence. Since that time, we have pursued a credible hunger to continue to experience many marking moments of His presence. This is entirely possible if we continue to pursue yet another level of desperation.

Ask God every day for another desperation. It is permissible. It is attainable. It is biblical. "Keep on asking and it will be given you; keep on seeking and you will find; keep on knocking [reverently] and [the door] will be opened to you" (Matthew 7:7 AMPC). Keep on. Don't relent, and never settle for less.

The first song that our worship team wrote in the revival is called "Desperate." I leave you with these words as you continue your journey of passionate spiritual pursuit and personal revival. May this sacred pilgrimage be filled with a growing intensity of desperation for Him.

Desperate

There's a longing in my soul that cannot be satisfied,
there's a burning in my spirit I cannot ignore.
Holy Father, hear our cry. We cry for more. Break
    open the Heavens. Send revival to Your Church
    and heal our land. Break open the Heavens.
We are desperate. We are desperate for more of Your
    Spirit, Your Spirit.
There's a fire deep inside, come and fan the flame,
    intensify Your Spirit in me. The closer that I get to
    You, the more of You I need. It's You I need.
We are desperate. We are desperate for more of Your
    Spirit, Your Spirit.
Oh, break open the Heavens!

Fresh Start Church Revival Worship

"Oh, that You would rend the heavens! That You would come down! That the mountains might shake at Your presence" (Isaiah 64:1).

ACKNOWLEDGMENTS

The writing of the book could not have been possible without the obedience, loyalty, inspiration, and demonstration of spiritual pursuit found in the company of revivalists at our church in Arizona, Fresh Start Church. Since we first saw the visitation of revival in 2015, we have experienced an inordinate and sustained sound of hunger and desperation resonating that has continued to the present day. This has happened first within our hearts and then flowed into a region and nation. It truly is an anomaly. My heart is full of righteous honor and gratitude for our church's dedication and surrender to birth and sustain personal and corporate revival. Thank you, Fresh Start Church, young and old, for your passionate pursuit of God and for being unwavering in your cry of desperation. You have inspired me, and you have inspired nations. Until Jesus returns—sustain revival.

NOTES

Chapter 1 The Power and Priority of the Place Called Secret

1. Gipsy Smith quoted by Brian Najapfour, "Our Nation's Greatest Need Is Revival," *The Aquila Report*, March 5, 2023, https://theaquila report.com/our-nations-greatest-need-is-revival.

Chapter 2 Where Are You? Revival Is a Walk!

1. *The Revival Study Bible*, ed. Steve Hill, William Pratney, and Tamara S. Winslow (Genesis Books, 2010), 1649.

2. James Strong, *Strong's Exhaustive Concordance of the Bible* (Thomas Nelson, 1990), under "H1980 halak," "G4043 peripateo."

3. Hailey, "Exercise Wheel Addiction in Hamsters," Hailey's Hamsters, January 30, 2021, http://haileyshamsters.com/exercise-wheel-add iction-in-hamsters.

Chapter 3 The Revelation of More

1. A. W. Tozer, *The Pursuit of God* (Aneko Press, 2015), 5.

2. Kim Owens, *Doorkeepers of Revival* (Destiny Image, 2021), 11.

3. Jannes Smith (John Smith), "A Doorkeeper in the House of My God," *Clarion* 61, no. 23 (2012): 572, https://clarionmagazine.ca/archives /2012/565-592_v61n23.pdf.

4. D. A. Carson, *The Expositor's Bible Commentary: Matthew*, ed. Frank Gaebelein (Zondervan, 1984), 513.

5. "What Is the Meaning of the Parable of the Ten Virgins?," Got Questions Ministries, page last updated January 4, 2022, https://www .gotquestions.org/parable-ten-virgins.html.

Chapter 4 The Eternal Pull—the Case for Personal Revival

1. *Mere Christianity* by CS Lewis © copyright 1942, 1943, 1944, 1952 CS Lewis Pte Ltd. Extract used with permission.

2. Wade E. Taylor, *Being Made Ready: A Daily Devotional; The Outpouring of Our Part in the Millennial Kingdom of God* (pub. by author, 2014), 54–55; italics in the original.

Chapter 5 Joined to the Lord

1. "What Is the Significance of High Places in the Bible?," Got Questions Ministries, page last updated January 4, 2022, https://www.gotquestions.org/high-places.html.

2. David Palmer, "Jesus Is the Bridegroom, We Are His Betrothed," LinkedIn, June 28, 2022, https://www.linkedin.com/pulse/jesus-bridegroom-we-his-betrothed-david-palmer.

3. Sheila A. Lewine, "Do You Have Any High Places?," The Way of the Word, September 21, 2022, https://sheilaalewine.com/2022/09/21/do-you-have-any-high-places.

4. Rick Renner, "The Holy Spirit Earnestly Yearns for You!," Renner, accessed November 20, 2024, https://renner.org/article/the-holy-spirit-earnestly-yearns-for-you.

5. "What Is the Significance of God Saying, 'I Will Betroth You to Me Forever' (Hosea 2:19)?," Got Questions Ministries, page last updated March 28, 2023, https://www.gotquestions.org/I-will-betroth-you-to-me-forever.html.

6. *The Revival Study Bible*, ed. Steve Hill, William Pratney, and Tamara S. Winslow (Genesis Books, 2010), 888.

Chapter 6 Deliverance unto Overcoming

1. "Strongholds" on Max Lucado's official website, September 2015, https://maxlucado.com/strongholds.

Chapter 7 The Cycle of Revival

1. "Hineni: Here I Am," Hebrew Word Lessons, January 26, 2020, https://hebrewwordlessons.com/2020/01/26/hineni-here-i-am.

2. *The Revival Study Bible*, ed. Steve Hill, William Pratney, and Tamara S. Winslow (Genesis Books, 2010), 1000.

3. Charles G. Finney, *Finney on Revival* (Bridge-Logos, 2014), back cover.

Chapter 8 The Necessity of Tongues

1. Corey Russell, *The Glory Within: The Interior Life and the Power of Speaking in Tongues* (Destiny Image, 2012), 73, 79.
2. Russell, *Glory Within*, 7, 76.

Chapter 9 The Burning Place

1. Mendy Kaminker, "The Showbread: The How and Why of the Temple Bread Offering," Chabad.org, accessed November 20, 2024, https://www.chabad.org/library/article_cdo/aid/2974301/jewish/The-Showbread-The-How-and-Why-of-the-Temple-Bread-Offering.htm.
2. Attributed to John Donne by Charles Spurgeon, *A Treasury of David*, vol. 6, *Psalm CXIX to CXXIV* (New York: 1882), 41.

Chapter 10 Deep Calls unto Deep

1. *Brown-Driver-Briggs Hebrew and English Lexicon*, "8415. tehom," Bible Hub, accessed November 20, 2024, https://biblehub.com/hebrew/8415.htm.
2. "How Does Pressure Impact Animals in the Ocean?," NOAA Ocean Exploration, accessed November 22, 2024, https://oceanexplorer.noaa.gov/facts/animal-pressure.html.
3. Blue Letter Bible, "thlipsis" (Strong's G2347), accessed November 22, 2024, https://www.blueletterbible.org/lexicon/g2347/kjv/tr/0-1.
4. Joyce Meyer (@JoyceMeyer), "We can't control what other people do and how they decide to treat us, but we can control our response to them," Twitter (now X), November 4, 2017, https://x.com/JoyceMeyer/status/926978624422600706.

Chapter 11 The Stairway of Ascent

1. Helen H. Lemmel, "Turn Your Eyes upon Jesus," 1922, public domain, https://hymnary.org/text/o_soul_are_you_weary_and_troubled.
2. Charles H. Spurgeon, "November 19 Evening," *Morning and Evening: A New Edition of the Classic Devotional Based on the Holy Bible, English Standard Version*, ed. Alistair Begg (Crossway Books, 2003).

Chapter 12 A Heart Set on a Pilgrimage

1. Ruth Ward Heflin, *Experiencing the Atmosphere of Heaven* (McDougal Publishing, 1990), introduction.

KIM OWENS, along with her husband, Paul, have been the senior pastors of Fresh Start Church in Peoria, Arizona, since 1997. It is a multicultural, multigenerational church where revival fire burns, the truth of God's Word is boldly proclaimed, and lives are transformed through the manifest presence of God and the power of the Holy Spirit. They have been experiencing sustained revival since 2015 and continue to cultivate revival moving forward. Pastor Kim is known for her high-impact, straightforward messages. Preaching and teaching as a firebrand with divine revelation, she brings life to the Word of God and a hunger for more of His presence.

Connect with Kim:

- DoorKeepersOfRevival.com
- FreshStartAZ.com
- /Kim.Owens.52687506
- @KimberlySOwens

www.ingramcontent.com/pod-product-compliance
Lightning Source LLC
Chambersburg PA
CBHW070342100426
42812CB00005B/1397